BUS FROM BA

'This book is a real page-turner! Although centred mainly in Thailand, the storyline also shuttles between South Africa, Lesotho, Malawi, Singapore, Malaysia and England and at every stage is firmly anchored in the providence of God in his dealings with two medical missionaries. Dorothy Rose's closely observed narrative is laced with gentle humour yet shot through with incidents faithfully reflecting the doubts and fear she and her husband Eddie faced, and gratefully recording God's remarkable answers to their prayers. Their story is charming and challenging, readable and relevant and a stirring call to wholehearted and obedient Christian commitment.'

Dr John Blanchard

'The perseverance and pleasure that characterise this couple's mission service is as relevant today as it was then. Though OMF's strategies and structures have changed to meet new challenges in East Asia, Eddie and Dorothy model the Christian maturity and cross-cultural skill with which OMF has always aspired to plant churches and work in partnership with local Christians there. Their life-long faith adventure, experiencing God's grace in all circumstances, is also profoundly encouraging for all Christians whether our place of service is in another culture or at home.'

Chris Wigram, National Director,
OMF International (UK)

'This account of ordinary missionary life abounds in extra-ordinary stories of God's providence at work when faith and obedience go together. Honesty and humour mingle in a story that holds you throughout.'

Philip H. Hacking
(ex chairman of Keswick Convention)

'Dorothy and Eddie Rose showed in their lives how faith and commitment to God never goes unrewarded (though not always in the way we may anticipate). Their fruitfulness in spreading the Gospel will be to their eternal credit. This book by Dorothy Rose is a fitting tribute to their lives and an inspiration to us all.'

David Wheatley,
British Heart Foundation Professor of Cardiac Surgery

Bus From Bangkok

DOROTHY ROSE

KINGSWAY PUBLICATIONS
EASTBOURNE

ISBN 1 84291 263 1
ISBN–13: 978–1–842912–63–8

01 02 03 04 05 Printing/Year 09 08 07 06

KINGSWAY COMMUNICATIONS LTD
Lottbridge Drove, Eastbourne BN23 6NT, England.
Email: books@kingsway.co.uk
Printed in the USA

Contents

CONTENTS

Thailand, showing positions of Bangkok, Manorom, Hat
Yai and Trang

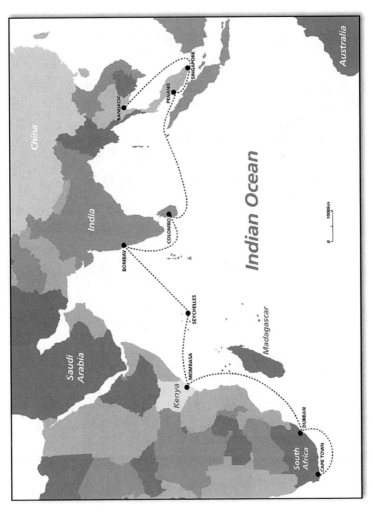

The Voyage from Cape Town to Singapore, and Singapore to Bangkok

Foreword

I first met Dorothy and Eddie Rose when they came to Glasgow to visit their daughter Susan. She was a nurse at the Royal Infirmary then, and worshipped with us at St George's-Tron Church.

My first impression was of people of outstanding quality spiritually, intellectually and professionally. That impression deepened as I got to know them better. As I have read Dorothy's remarkable book, I have realised that their missionary career was infinitely more exciting than I knew.

This is one of those books of which people will genuinely say, 'I just could not put it down.' That is partly because Dorothy is a natural storyteller, with a vivid, lively style. But it is also because the events themselves are so remarkable and captivating – at times astonishing and at times quite hilarious.

The book is full of riveting lessons and examples of God's unchanging faithfulness in every kind of situation.

I am so glad that Dorothy has devoted all the time and hard work to put this excellent material into written form. I anticipate that the book will be widely read, and have no doubt that it will bring lasting blessing to those who read it.

Eric J. Alexander
Formerly minister of St George's-Tron Church, Glasgow

Preface

The early winter winds are gusting madly round the garden, stripping dry brown leaves from the trees and leaving the sadly bare branches reaching up hopelessly to the bleak grey sky. Even though I am dressed warmly I feel chilled as I sit typing in 'sunny South Africa'. Whether this winter is indeed colder than any I remember from the past, or whether I simply feel it more because it is only a few years since we returned from living in Southeast Asia, is not important to me; what is of more concern is the lurking conviction that haunts me, illogical though it is, that I will never really be warm again!

Will I ever be able to recall that feeling of warmth that was always with us when we lived in Thailand, always steamy with heat and humidity and yet brilliant in the harsh tropical sunshine? No muted pastel colours there; hues were garish, flamboyant and uninhibited. The background to any scene clamoured for attention as much as the foreground. In that scorching land even the simple act of walking was not simple any more – especially at the time of the monsoon, when it felt as though one was wading through knee-deep water, so solid was the moisture-laden air.

The years we spent in South-east Asia have left an indelible mark on us. The small and graceful people of Thailand with their gentle and insidiously attractive culture have made their imprint on our lives and our personalities and we will never be quite the same again.

Come with Me to Thailand. . .

For he said, 'I have been a stranger in a foreign land.'

(Exodus 2:22)

Life for us in Thailand was very different from life in South Africa. During the first few weeks we were in Bangkok we felt as if it would be impossible to live there. When we walked side by side on the uneven pavements of the city we could not have any conversation, due to the continuous roar of the passing traffic – day or night. There was no running hot water, so we had to shower in 'cold' water that was actually tepid because of the searing heat. Everything seemed a little harder in Thailand than it did at home, so that living there was rather like trying to run with your feet buried in clinging sand.

My husband Eddie once told me that life in Thailand was 'like living in Wonderland, like Alice', and that to drive down a one-way street and find cars or motorbikes coming towards you was like being at the Mad Hatter's tea party. In Thailand a green traffic light does not always mean you have right of way. When we came to an intersection, we always had to slow down and look left and right before crossing in case a vehicle should disregard the red light and come right into our path. As a Thai friend once told us, 'We have rules and traffic lights just as the West has – but in abnormal conditions we don't have to obey them!'

In the West it is efficiency that is prized. But in Thailand good relationships with others are valued more. It is far more important not to cause others to be embarrassed than to be efficient. We were told that when a man makes an appointment with someone of higher status, he should never be punctual. *Why not?* we wondered. Our Thai friend smiled as he told us the obvious: should the senior person be delayed, he would certainly lose face if the junior were already there waiting when he arrived. We also found out that time in Thailand is not adhered to as it is in the West. Whenever we made an arrangement to meet a Thai friend we had to find out if he was thinking of 'Thai time' or '*farang*[1] time'. If we forgot to do that, we could easily find ourselves waiting fruitlessly for two or more hours before our friend turned up.

In spite of being so different from the West, Thailand is a fascinating and captivating land. Nothing is ever simple. We soon learned to relax and accept whatever should happen. Let me explain by inviting you to come with me on an ordinary bus trip from the capital Bangkok to Manorom in Central Thailand. How can simply sitting in a bus introduce anyone to the vagaries of Thai society? Climb on board with me for this journey of 240 kilometres and you will get a fairly good idea of how in Thailand even apparently straightforward things have a way of becoming complicated.

---

[1] 'Foreigner'.

It is mid-afternoon. After a hot ride in an open *tuk-tuk*,[2] we reach the northern bus station, swarming with people who are all talking at once. All available benches are occupied and there are no fans to move the hot and heavy air. As we stand in the throng waiting for our bus to arrive, my heart sinks as I think of the cramped and stifling heat and discomfort that shortly will be ours for the next three to four hours. Our bus will not have air conditioning.

Eventually an ancient red bus arrives. We are fortunate that we have been allotted seats in the front, with plenty of room for our long legs. As we climb up the steps, some garlands of brightly coloured flowers catch our eyes as they hang from the roof in front of the windscreen, where they will sway and swing with the motion of the bus once it gets moving. In a row on top of the dashboard several small gold-painted images of Buddha proclaim the Thai national faith, and on the side of the windscreen is a triangular design of white dots. A Buddhist priest has applied these marks as a blessing of protection. No one ever loses faith in the priest's protective dots – although accidents in this land often involve head-on collisions at high speed that leave no survivors.

Once inside the bus we find a Buddhist nun in a white robe sitting on one of our seats with her parcels and plastic bags on the other. She smiles benignly and says disarmingly, '*Maj pen raj!*' (It doesn't matter). (It is only later that I learn there is an unspoken rule that a monk or nun may always sit in the roomy seats at the front of a bus.) We stand in the narrow aisle and I ask her to excuse me, saying, '*Kho thort*

---

[2] 'Motorbike taxi'.

kha!' (Please excuse me) as we wait for her to remove her belongings. The conductor comes up to us and, in deference to the nun, suggests that we could perhaps find seats at the back. I explain apologetically that the seats at the rear are very close together and that we *farangs* will not have sufficient legroom; that is the reason why we have reserved these particular places. Eventually the nun gathers her parcels together and leaves, letting us sink gratefully onto the hard, vinyl-covered seats.

The scheduled departure time of three o'clock comes and goes, but the bus remains in its place. Eventually the conductor takes a large screwdriver out of his short-sleeved shirt pocket and uses it to attach a trumpet-shaped object to the klaxon. This device will amplify the normal sound of the horn to produce the imperious blare that will intimidate all other vehicles on the road and cause them to scurry out of the path of the bus. Seeing this sign of imminent departure, a young Thai girl, realising that she is thirsty, gets up from her seat, explaining to the conductor that she wants to leave the bus to buy a cool drink. He nods to her and she leaves the bus. But she stays away longer than she should have and eventually the driver impatiently reverses the bus out of its allotted parking bay, ready to leave as soon as she returns. He motions to the conductor to go to fetch her. When at last the girl appears, she is smiling broadly, apparently completely unconcerned that she has delayed the bus. (Later we learn that the Thai react to feelings of embarrassment by smiling.)

By this time my legroom has shrunk. Four teenage youths are seated on the engine cover, directly in front of my seat. It is awkward, and I hardly know where to put my feet. I cannot let my feet touch the youths, as I have learnt that it is a profound insult to touch another person with one's feet. The Thai revere the head as holy, while the feet are the least honourable part of the body. This principle is of such great importance that before a doctor can even touch a patient's head during a medical examination, he or she must ask the patient's permission.

At last our bus moves off, but it is not yet able to leave the bus station courtyard. First it has to weave its way between other buses parked at all angles in the crowded yard. We twist and turn on our way to the exit. Suddenly a gleaming smart blue air-conditioned tour bus dashes in front of us to cut us off. It is evidently a familiar game to the two drivers. The driver of our old red battered bus refuses to be intimidated or to give way or slow down. The tour bus driver slams on his brakes with a loud *whoosh!* He feels no rancour at all, acknowledging defeat with a cheery wave of his hand. Once in the exit gap, we wait for a chance to slip in between the seemingly never-ending line of traffic, our engine racing. At last our driver sees his chance and squeezes into the slow-moving procession. As we crawl along, inch by inch, I happen to glance down at the floor and notice several gaps in the flooring of the old bus. I realise with surprise that I can see the uneven surface of the road passing under us.

Taking advantage of our lack of speed, our conductor stands up, opens the door and quickly leaps off the moving bus, all in one brisk movement. Fascinated, we watch him as he crosses the street, wary of wayward motorbikes, and disappears into a tiny shop. He soon reappears, a plastic bag of curry and rice swinging from his hand, and boards the bus again, knowing that he will not have to go hungry during the trip.

Eventually we draw near to the six-lane highway that will take us past the international airport and further northwards to Central Thailand. When we are only a short distance from the highway our bus is forced to come to an unexpected stop, as a car is parked directly in its path. Its driver remains sitting in his vehicle until the passenger he has brought has successfully boarded the bus immediately behind ours. Nobody seems to mind. The imperturbable Thai accept this delay philosophically.

For the first part of the broad highway the bus stops at regular intervals. Each time the conductor leans dangerously out of the open door to call out to those standing there, inviting more people to come with us. Finally our bus is *really* packed, all seats taken and passengers standing shoulder to shoulder in the aisle. This is the first time I realise that in Thailand a bus is considered full only when there is no standing room left in the aisle and even more passengers stand, half in and half out of the doorway. Past the airport we thunder, every part of the old bus shaking and protesting with creaks and groans.

Unexpectedly, a traffic jam looms ahead, involving four lanes of traffic. Our driver does not hesitate. Without reducing speed at all, he wrenches his steering wheel violently to the left and careers along the road's sloping grassy verge past all the other stationary vehicles. Other cars and motorbikes follow his example. The surface of the verge becomes more and more uneven and one by one the other vehicles leave it and re-enter the queue of traffic, satisfied to have gained some little advantage. But even though the verge becomes a sandy ridge, our driver keeps on his course and the bus mounts this small hill, tilting and teetering, until soon it finds a more level path again. We continue in this manner, gaily passing the long line of traffic, until we find an enormous lorry stopped in front of us. It can advance no more as the buttress of a bridge takes up the entire verge. It is waiting until it can insinuate its bulk between two vehicles in the long, sluggish stream of crawling traffic. We stop behind it until it has succeeded and then follow its example. Even in these trying circumstances, no driver hoots or shows signs of impatience. This is Thailand, the land of the *caj jen*,[3] where no one shows signs of stress no matter what frustration should plague them. Like Dickens' Mr Micawber, they all wait patiently for 'something to turn up'.

A few miles on, we come to another traffic jam. A gargantuan truck, laden to the skies with enormous sacks of rice, has broken down and is blocking all three lanes of the highway. In time-honoured Thai tradition its driver has absconded in an attempt to avoid blame. It is still too soon for the traffic police to have arrived, with their shrill whistles and imperious gestures. The enterprising Thai drivers, however, do not stop for long. Again they make use of the narrow verge at the side of the road.

By this time almost two hours have passed, and we are only about 40 kilometres from Bangkok – with a long way still to go. The sun beats down with relentless heat, even though its rays are now more slanted and the shadows have grown longer. Suddenly, without warning, a little old Thai lady walks casually across the highway in front of us,

---

[3] Cool heart.

apparently unaware of her imminent danger. Our bus shudders to a halt inches from her stooped form. Even then she does not look up. She is probably deaf and half blind. Our driver shrugs slightly, giving no other sign of irritation or frustration.

From time to time vendors take the opportunity that presents itself whenever the bus slows down, jumping agilely aboard the moving vehicle. They ride with us for a short while, squeezing their way up and down the crowded aisle while balancing reed trays of food and drink on one hand. They offer fizzy drinks in plastic bags with crushed ice, miserable dry pieces of charcoal-grilled saffron-yellow chicken, little rice cakes and sweet or savoury dumplings. For a *farang* to eat one of these dumplings would be disastrous, as they have been cooked some time ago and exposed to the air. Not having the immunity of the Thai, we will almost certainly experience severe dysentery should we eat them. Their trays empty, the vendors wait near the door ready to jump nimbly from the bus whenever its speed slackens.

As the highway becomes less congested, the whine of our engine increases steadily and triumphantly as we speed up to pass all the other vehicles in front of us. Trucks, tankers, overcrowded minibuses – it seems that none can compete with us. Sometimes there is very little room to spare, but we pass them just the same. Occasionally we stop to let a passenger alight and each time the vehicles we have just passed come up and overtake us one by one. But what fun to dash off again after them, catch them up and pass them all over again! While passing, our driver resolutely keeps the bus on the wrong side of the road: he knows that any other vehicle that happens to be approaching us will swerve off the road on to the verge. The rule of the road in Thailand is that the larger the vehicle, the more clout it has on the road. As for the few that will *not* give way, their eloquent wrecks line the highway. Through the window we see the wreck of a bus, lying on its side in the canal that runs next to the road. Nonchalant passengers perch on top, squeezing out their wet clothes and spreading them on the surface of the bus to dry in the sun.

All this time a television screen flickers, placed high in the front of the bus. The conductor is responsible for choosing and loading the videotapes, and we soon realise that he enjoys movies full of violence and magic, with actors flying through the air and performing marvellous feats.

The bus shudders once more to a halt. This time it is not to let a passenger off. Through the side windows we passengers can see dense black smoke billowing upwards. As some of the smoke enters the bus, the unpleasant odour of burning rubber comes with it. The conductor hops down the steps to look. He reports to the driver that loose stones on the road have shredded some of the rubber of the left rear tyre. Unfortunately, we do not have a spare. When he and the driver, after much discussion, decide to continue the journey, they try to reassure each other that the tyre should last long enough. It is at this stage that I begin to pray earnestly for our safety during the rest of the journey. The light is now fading rapidly.

Without any warning, the driver veers off the road and steers the bus into the yard of a petrol station. This is not because he needs petrol, but rather to allow us passengers out to buy food and drinks if we so wish. The driver and conductor remain in the bus, as they have a large, wide-mouthed thermos container filled with crushed ice in a recess to the left of the driver's seat. As time passes, the ice melts steadily, so they always have ice-cold water to drink. Both men share the one grubby plastic mug attached to the thermos by a twist of pink raffia.

By now the bus is half empty. A woman sitting across the aisle from me has noticed that the engine cover is unoccupied. She politely removes her blue plastic sandals and then stretches out her legs so that her feet can rest on top of the cover. The conductor has switched off the television at the end of the last film and now the radio is on for the news. Unfortunately, shrill conversations between some women passengers, from one side of the bus to the other, are drowning out the sound of the news presenter. Outside the bus it is now pitch dark. The lights from oncoming vehicles are blinding. But our driver knows he is invincible on the road: however strong the oncoming beams of light, the extra-bright beams of the bus make them seem as weak as candlelight. In Thailand it is almost unknown for drivers to dip their bright lights as a courtesy to oncoming traffic. Thank goodness we are in the bus – its lights outshine all others!

When the bus turns sharply off the great Asian Highway onto a narrow road, I know I am nearly at Manorom. Although the surface of this road is pitted with potholes, our speed hardly slackens. Our driver is aware that our bus is larger than almost any other vehicle he can meet on this road and therefore, should there be a collision, the bus would be victorious.

After about 15 kilometres on this country road, the bus

obediently grinds to a halt to let us off at the mouth of the lane that leads to the front entrance of Manorom Christian Hospital. We are exhausted from the long journey, but our fatigue soon dissipates as we realise with relief that this particular adventure has finally come to an end, and we are there at last.

1
The Start of It All

For so it was commanded me by the word of the
LORD. . .

(1 Kings 13:9)

O ur lives changed radically in 1964. At that time
Eddie and I, both medical doctors, were living and
practising in the busy Karroo town of Oudtshoorn,
South Africa. We had moved there from Cape Town in
order for Eddie, a consultant general surgeon, to acquire
good experience in a group general practice prior to setting
up his own specialist surgical practice.

We had been married for seven years and had four children (two boys followed by two girls). At first, though importuned by Professor James Louw to continue working for him
after my marriage, I stayed at home to bring up our family
and to support Eddie in his extremely busy and demanding
years at Groote Schuur Hospital while he worked as a surgical registrar, rotating through various divisions such as general surgery, paediatric surgery, neurosurgery, orthopaedics
and trauma surgery. During these early years in Cape Town
Eddie was stretched near to breaking point, with sleepless
nights on call and long, long days that often started at dawn,
while he received a pittance of a salary that demanded all
my innovation and economising in order to manage.

One bonus of our work experience after qualifying was that we had the privilege of working with Professor Christian Barnard. He was Eddie's registrar when Eddie was an intern in the City Infectious Fevers Hospital. There Eddie learned to respect Chris's zeal and single mindedness and his indefatigable appetite for work – and even the way Chris demanded the same high standard of work from him, night and day. At that time I was still a fifth-year medical student, but eventually I also worked with Chris for my surgical registrar. We interns, overawed by his reputation and fame, treated the great man with respect and kept our distance. His reputation was not only due to his fantastic research and his achievement of the world's first heart transplant, but also due to his freely given appreciation of the fairer sex. We women interns preferred to climb the stairs if he was the sole occupant of a lift.

The three-doctor practice in Oudtshoorn was thriving and we wanted for nothing. We had a gracious, well-furnished home with a swimming pool and a large garage. Life flowed smoothly about us – until some words began to disturb and haunt us. It was Eddie who first heard these words and, thereafter, could not get them out of his mind.

One Sunday, while I looked after the children at home, he went to the evening church service. During the service the minister quoted a sentence that caught and held Eddie's attention: 'For whoever desires to save his life will lose it, but whoever loses his life for My sake will find it' (Matthew 16:25). Although the words were very familiar to him, they came with a fresh impact. When the service ended they were still ringing in his ears. Eddie could not forget those words. They seemed to be aimed right at him. *Am I not saving my life?* he thought. In Oudtshoorn we had a good life, plenty of money and three cars, and he had an enviable reputation as a good doctor and surgeon. Each time he had occasion to walk down the main street of the town he was greeted by all who saw him. He was highly respected, fulfilled in his medical work and extremely happy at home. Could God be calling him to give up that full and happy life? Was he meant to lose it all for God?

We had always hoped to be medical missionaries some day, and some years previously we had applied to the Overseas Missionary Fellowship. We had been unsuccessful as I was pregnant with our second child and at that time the OMF had a policy of not accepting missionary candidates if they had more than one child. Now we had four! And we were so settled and happy. Eddie's mind seethed with half-formed ideas. He examined the possibility of exchanging his rewarding private practice for the austere life of a missionary doctor. We could face personal discomfort and loss of income, but what about our children? He knew that Thailand was the only country in which OMF had medical work. He also knew that hot and humid Thailand was not a healthy place for young children. *We would have to leave our children behind in the care of others!* came the unwelcome thought. Then he prayed, *No, Lord, we can't do that. You gave the children into our care. They are our responsibility.*

For the next three Sundays, without explaining why, Eddie attended evening services at other churches. He was scared he might hear those words from Matthew's Gospel again. What a shock it was for him, therefore, to hear the identical verse quoted each time. He said nothing to me about all this, but kept the perplexing problem in his heart.

One morning, as he was reading his Bible during his

regular quiet time, he came across these words of the prophet Isaiah, describing the Messiah: 'And His name will be called Wonderful, Counselor, Mighty God, Everlasting Father, Prince of Peace' (Isaiah 9:6). When Eddie read the words 'Everlasting Father', he could go no further. He knelt down and prayed. Straight away it was as if the Lord spoke to him about the children: *Eddie, if you died today, would you be happy to trust your children to Me?* Eddie's immediate response was, *Yes, of course, Lord.* And he felt God say, *Then why won't you trust Me with them now, while you are still alive?*

Eddie was left without words. Then he prayed in desperation, *Lord, I don't understand. Other Christian folk won't understand either!* The Lord replied, *Yes, Eddie, but I'm not asking others to do this – just you. Trust Me!*

Eddie realised it was simply a matter of trusting in God rather than in his own strength. He came to me and told me all that had happened and we prayed together, making up our minds to obey God's call and trust Him to look after the children.

We sent in our applications to OMF, and as soon as we heard from the South African OMF Council that they were unanimous in recommending our acceptance to the mission field, we gave notice to the other partners in the medical practice and sold our home. While we waited for our applications to be processed at OMF Headquarters in Singapore, we responded to an SOS for doctors to be sent out from a small mission hospital in a town called Thaba 'Nchu, very near Lesotho. We expected to be available to work there for about six months, by which time we should have received the answer to our applications from Singapore.

2

Thaba 'Nchu

But this He said to test him, for He Himself knew
what He would do.

(John 6:6)

The Moroka Mission Hospital stood on the outskirts of
Thaba 'Nchu. Because it had been built near the border of the mountainous little country of Lesotho, it
served both the Basotho and the Tswana people. We
quickly picked up a smattering of Southern Sotho, enough
to communicate with the patients and staff. This was the
language most commonly spoken and even those who did
not speak it were able to understand it.

For our young family Thaba 'Nchu was paradise. The two
boys climbed on the roof of the garage and played cops and
robbers inside the old hedge that bordered our garden. Both
they and their older sister took turns to steal rides on hospital trolleys up and down the sloping passages between the
wards. The nurses adored them and spoiled them. Our
youngest daughter was only six months old when we arrived, so she could not take an active part in the lively play.

Only once were the children taken by surprise by the

Tswana, Zulu and Basotho nurses. It was Jennifer's fifth birthday and I had planned a party for the children after school. I had also invited any nurses who were off duty to come to the party. I had baked plenty of treats and had just finished setting the table when I was surprised to find a happy contingent of nurses, eager to come to the party. The fact that the birthday girl was not yet there made no difference to them. They milled about the table, eating and drinking with abandon. As I invited them to help themselves from the overflowing plates of cake, scones and other treats, I learned (to my cost) of a cultural difference between us. We had always been used to taking one cake or biscuit at a time before taking another. To these girls, it was polite to take one piece of *everything* that was available before they retreated from the table to eat the good things that crowded their plates. You can imagine what happened: long before the children returned from school, the table was bare of everything except crumbs. As soon as the nurses left, effusive in their thanks and appreciation, I was busy in the kitchen again, whipping up some more quick goodies for Jennifer and the other children.

In the hospital the small outpatient area seemed always to be full to overflowing. In spite of this we found that the people, young and old, were almost always ready to wait their turn. Their good-humoured patience was an example to us doctors and nurses. One day a young man of about 30 told me earnestly, 'I am troubled by a large snake inside my stomach!' Masking my surprise, I examined him on the couch. As I palpated his abdomen I found that his colon was very full and realised that he had been constipated for quite some time. Normal movement in the large bowel was exaggerated and he interpreted this as the movements of a 'snake'. I arranged for him to be admitted to the ward for treatment. However, as he believed firmly in the 'snake' inside his abdomen, I knew he would not easily be able to accept a standard regimen of treatment for constipation of long duration. So, going to the hospital pharmacy armed with an empty orange squash bottle, I took some Epsom salts, mixed it with a bright green tonic, added a few vitamins and other harmless ingredients and shook them all together in the bottle. This I took to the young man in the ward. I told him I would leave the bottle on the locker next to his bed so that it would be available to him, and every time he felt the 'snake' move in his abdomen, he should take a mouthful of the virulent-looking mixture.

'But I always thought that in a hospital the nurses must bring the medicine to the patients!' he protested.

'Ah, but your case is different,' I told him. 'You are the only one who will know when the "snake" moves. How would the nurses know when to give you some medicine?'

He agreed to this, and lay back in his bed. When we made rounds in that ward, he was silent when we came to his bed, but sat up and indicated with his hands held apart the size of the 'snake'. Day by day his hands were closer together and his smile grew broader. One day his hands were clasped together: the 'snake' had shrivelled up completely and he was cured!

One morning, not long after we had arrived in Thaba 'Nchu, a woman came forward holding a baby boy close to her breast. When Eddie examined the child he found he was *in extremis*. 'Your baby is dying. Why did you not bring him sooner?' he asked.

'I took him first to the witch doctor,' she replied. 'Then, when I saw he was getting no better, I thought I should bring the baby here.'

The mother's reply came as a shock. We had not realised the strength of the hold that the local witch doctor had over the people. When the baby first became ill the mother had called the witch doctor to her hut to treat him. In spite of the 'treatment', the child's condition deteriorated steadily. When the mother suggested she take the baby to the mission hospital, the witch doctor became angry. He went outside the hut, took a stick and drew a circle in the ground all around the hut. 'You'd better not take the baby out of the circle,' he warned solemnly, 'or he will die!'

Frightened out of her wits, the mother kept the baby in the hut for another two days. At last, seeing the marked worsening in her baby's condition, she dared take him out of the hut, crossed the line and ran to the mission hospital to see the doctor. Unfortunately, by this time it was too late to save the baby. When the mother returned home, disconsolate and mourning, the witch doctor was triumphant: by delaying hospital treatment with his threats, he had caused the hospital to be blamed for the child's death.

Another grim example of the power of the witch doctor among the people served by the hospital was that of a lovely 17-year-old girl. Her mother brought her to the outpatient department because she was listless and unwilling to eat. She told us that a witch doctor had placed a spell on the girl and that she was going to die because of it. She had brought her daughter to the mission hospital as a last resort.

The girl was pleasant and amenable in the ward to which she had been admitted, but she ate hardly anything and grew weaker by the day. We did all the tests we could, but neither they nor repeated examinations revealed any physical abnormality in the girl. I had never experienced anything like this before and I railed against the seemingly inevitable deterioration in her physical condition. Was there *nothing* we could do to fight this belief in the witch doctor's magic? We were giving her intravenous feeding and vitamins by injection – but they did not help at all. The girl had surrendered to the fixed belief that she must die because of the witch doctor's curse. Inevitably she sank into a coma, and in a matter of weeks she was dead.

Witchcraft, magic spells and curses were ubiquitous. A young Mosotho girl called Berta came daily to help look after and amuse our children. She was short, plump and very good natured and her cheery smiles quickly made her a favourite with them. When she had to leave again they missed her at first, of course, but with the resilience of youngsters it was not long before they were happily playing among themselves. One afternoon some months later, a strange young woman came to our gate, stood outside and called for me. As I drew near I saw that she had Berta with her. I greeted Berta, but she did not respond. Her friend soon explained that Berta could not speak. Ever since she had attended a meeting the previous evening she had not been able to utter a sound. On questioning her further, I found out that the meeting was one of a notorious sect, popular in that area of Thaba 'Nchu. At these meetings there were always some in the congregation who became 'possessed' and danced about, shrieking vociferously. But for Berta, the meeting had left her absolutely dumb. The girl told me she had brought Berta to me so that I could pray over her and she might be healed. (It seemed really strange to me that she had brought Berta to the mission hospital for her healing, when the sect was absolutely opposed to traditional Christianity.)

I opened the gate and let Berta in, but felt obliged to ask the friend to wait outside the gate as her eyes looked so evil. I took Berta to our bedroom and we shut our eyes in preparation for prayer. Immediately I was overcome with trepidation. What if I prayed and the Lord did not heal her? All the ramifications of such a failure filled my mind. But then I put my trust in God, asking Him to hear my prayer for the sake of Christ Jesus, His Son and my Saviour, and to heal Berta and enable her to speak once more. The Lord wonderfully answered that prayer, and as Berta opened her eyes again she uttered a sound – a meaningless noise, but at least it was a sound. Then she began to speak. Her voice was scratchy and guttural, but it was certainly intelligible. She bowed her head again as I prayed in gratitude to God.

As we went out to the gate I warned Berta against attending meetings of this demonic sect and pleaded with her to attend her family's church instead. She said she would do that, but some weeks later she was back outside our gate with the same friend – again unable to speak. The night before she had been at another meeting of the same sect. Once more I took her inside and prayed earnestly and humbly for mercy from the Lord that she might be able to speak again. When I had finished the prayer she made a croaking sound as she tried to speak. After a few minutes the sounds became intelligible. I accompanied her to the gate as before, but advised her that she had better not attend the sect's meetings in the future. I felt I would not be able to pray for her again if she deliberately exposed herself to evil influences and was struck dumb a third time. I never saw Berta again after that, or even heard about her. I only hope she did decide to attend her family's church again rather than that exotic sect.

In stark contrast to the evil in the spirit world, we were privileged indeed to come to know Canon Michael Mohaleroe. He was a quiet, deep man of God, showing peace and tranquillity in his life whatever the circumstances. Michael was responsible for the Anglican church in Thaba 'Nchu, and came regularly to the hospital to minister communion to the nurses who were members of his church. He was wise and a source of much good advice to Eddie and me, especially at the start of our stay there. He told us not to worry that the house allocated to us by the Methodist church was a much nicer one than the homes of the people around us. I had wondered why we should live in such a comfortable house while so many others lived very much more simply. He replied that it was suitable for doctors to live in a better house and everyone would expect that – but that it would be a very good thing if our door was always open to anyone and a warm welcome extended to them. So we closed our door only at night and we found that the Tswana and Basotho men and women appreciated the fact that they could feel free to come in at any time. At night we did not even lock our door – one reason being that Michael Mohaleroe could come in at 4 a.m. without hindrance and make himself a cup of coffee before going on to the nearby town of Tweespruit to hold an early morning communion service.

One day Michael came to me and asked if I would be

willing to speak to a group of unmarried mothers from a doctor's point of view. These women would sit in front of the church on something called 'the penitents' bench' when they attended a service, until they had fulfilled the church's requirements and been restored to full fellowship. So one afternoon I went to the church and there sat five young women with serious faces. How was I to address them? It would need to be in a way that was understandable to them and not in a condescending 'holier than thou' fashion. I greeted them and was rewarded by cautious smiles. I can remember only one thing I told them that day, and that was to be careful in their relationships with men: 'If you have a hungry dog before you, you don't put a full plate of food in front of it unless you want it eaten up!'

The months passed quickly. One day a letter from Singapore arrived and we tore it open eagerly. What disappointment! What dismay! The OMF Headquarters in Singapore had rejected our application. We simply could not understand it. We had applied with the unanimous backing of the South African OMF Council. What could have gone wrong? We each took a deep breath and started to read the letter in its entirety instead of skimming it for its decision. The letter said that although OMF was in dire need of doctors for its hospitals in Thailand, the council members 'did not have the freedom of the Spirit' to accept our application. Eddie and I were devastated at first, and only with tears and much heart-searching and prayer did we feel at peace with their decision.

Some weeks earlier I had noticed that each evening when I sat up in bed to read before going to sleep, leaning against the headboard, a tender spot over my spine hurt me. I loved this time of quiet in the evening when I could read without interruption, so this tenderness was a source of irritation. As time went by, it did not go away, and the discomfort even increased. At that stage I had no idea that this troublesome tender spot was to lead to nearly four years of serious illness that almost cost me my life.

3

An Unexpected Turn

I saw visions of God.
(Ezekiel 1:1)

T he tenderness on my spine increased, causing me more and more discomfort, and I began to run a low-grade fever. Eddie finally took me to an orthopaedic surgeon, but after examination he could not be sure of the cause of my pain, and X-ray results did not yield a definite answer. I saw other doctors and had other tests. Worst of all was not knowing what was wrong with my back. This was the beginning of years of lying flat on my bed at home, alternating with weeks or months of hospitalisation. I could not stand up for more than a few minutes at a time. I lost so much weight that I looked skeletal and I was not strong enough to care for the children. I did not even have the strength to carry our young baby, Susan. When Doris Tamblyn, matron of the mission hospital, came to visit me she took one look at me and exclaimed, 'Dorothy, you must have committed a dreadful sin that you are suffering like this!' Needless to say, that remark did not help me at all.

Eddie and I were desperately in need of help in looking after our young family. No family members were in a position to assist. Finally we found people who cared enough to help. A middle-aged couple in Oudtshoorn, Carel and Miemie Babst, who had originally been Eddie's patients, had become very good friends. They offered to fetch our children and look after them until I was able to do so once more. With his mother-in-law, Ouma, Carel drove to Thaba 'Nchu (a distance of just over 800 kilometres) and took our four children back to Oudtshoorn. For the next three and a half years Carel and Miemie cared for the children as if they were their own, and that was a comfort to me.

I will always remember the day that a neurosurgeon and an orthopaedic surgeon finally decided to operate on my spine. They were not sure what they would find, so they invited Eddie to be present at the operation. They were taken aback to find in my spine two inches of diseased, necrotic bone, purplish in colour. 'Look at this!' they called to Eddie. 'Why didn't it show up on X-ray?' They removed the affected parts of the spine, leaving the spinal cord without its protective covering of bone. They tried to restore the spine's stability and give the cord a bony covering again by packing the area with bone chips taken from my pelvis. When I woke from the anaesthetic the pain I felt was made a little more bearable by the knowledge that at last the cause of my illness had been found and by the hope that I would now recover.

Unfortunately the spinal fusion was not a success. A hospital 'super bug' had been introduced into my body and I almost died from septicaemia (blood poisoning). The bone grafts died and had to be removed by further surgery. For almost a week I hovered between life and death. I was not really aware of what was happening – everything was hazy

to me. I was told later that my temperature was around
41.5°C (107°F). A good friend of ours was so concerned that
she paid for a private nurse to be with me every night during this time.

Eventually, I turned the corner and started to get well.
Finally, after five and a half months in hospital, I was
allowed home. Yes, I was home again, but I was not yet
well. The back pain and fever continued. My appetite had
not returned. Even though the wound in my back had
finally healed up, I was still bedridden and weak. Many
friends all over South Africa prayed for my healing, as did
our friends and colleagues at the mission hospital. But I
remained ill. I was a wreck – bedridden, always with a fever
and constant back pain.

Early one morning, as I was starting to read my Bible for
my quiet time, a disturbing thought flashed through my
mind. In spite of all the prayers from many friends in different parts of South Africa, I had not been healed. What if
it was not the Lord's will for me to be healed? I faced facts
then for the first time since the illness began. *If the Lord had
allowed me to become so ill for a special purpose of His own and did
not want me to get better, was I willing to accept suffering, pain and
disability from Him? Was I willing to 'die young' as a doctor had
suggested? Was I willing to trust His judgement and accept His will
for me even if it meant I could never again be a wife to Eddie, or a
mother to my children?* I faced up to the very real possibility
that this might indeed be what the Lord had chosen for me.
Finally, though it was a struggle, I yielded to His will. With
bowed head and tears running down my cheeks I finally
accepted whatever fate He had in store for me. As I did so,
a wonderful sense of peace flooded through me. We never

prayed for my healing again after that experience. After three years of agonised pleading we had peace, in spite of there being no improvement in my condition.

One afternoon some days later, I felt as if I could not get enough air. Fortunately Eddie was also in the room, as within a matter of minutes my breathing became increasingly shallow and soon I lay unconscious on the bed. Eddie grabbed the telephone next to the bed and phoned urgently for a nurse to bring over an anaesthetic machine and a cylinder of oxygen so that he could force some air into my lungs. By the time these arrived my pulse had already slowed to only twelve beats a minute and my pupils were dark and fully dilated – both signs of a severe lack of oxygen.

Rosalie Taylor, who was matron at that time, had come over to see if she could help. She, Eddie and Sister Winifred Mabece all pushed the bed away from the wall and squeezed the anaesthetic machine into the space between the wall and the bed. Eddie introduced an airway into my mouth and started breathing for me by pumping forcibly on the anaesthetic rebreathing bag. Rosalie sat by my bed, clasping my limp hands. The minutes ticked away inexorably, stretching into hours.

During this period of unconsciousness, I had a dream – or, rather, a vision.

I found myself in a large, dark, icy cave. Its walls were wet, slippery and cold. I felt so cold that I knew someone must have exchanged the blood in my veins for ice water. I was furious and wanted to find someone to whom I could complain. As I walked this way and that, the entrance to a tunnel opened up before me. I turned into this tunnel hoping it would lead me to a person who would listen to my grievance. Far ahead of me I could make out a faint glow. As I drew nearer the glow, I could see that in the tunnel's exit stood a figure. I cannot remember anything about that figure except for two things: first, I could not make out what He was wearing because He seemed to be surrounded by light, and second, although I could not make out any features other than His eyes, I did not care at all. My eyes were fixed on His and His eyes were full of love – such love as you cannot even imagine! A forgiving and unconditional love looked at me from those eyes. My heart swelled within me and all else but those eyes paled into utter insignificance and I responded to that love eagerly, longing with all my heart to stay near Him. I forgot my family. I forgot everything. Words spilled out of my mouth of their own volition: 'Lord, I am ready – may I come?' Gently He shook His head. 'No,' He replied, 'your children are still too young.'

The next thing I knew, I was back in my bedroom. As I opened my eyes, the matron, still holding my hands, spoke. 'Dorothy, why did you speak out loud just before you woke? You said, "Lord, I am ready – may I come?"'

That wonderful glimpse into heaven, of being in the very presence of the Lord, has changed my life for ever. Ever since that time, the thought of death has not frightened me. I no longer even think about what heaven will be like. I know I will be with the Lord, and nothing else could ever be better than simply being with Him, enfolded in His marvellous love.

For five or six more months my physical condition was unchanged. One day I realised something that completely took away the disappointment of the OMF decision not to accept our application. I was reading in John 6 about the feeding of the five thousand. Jesus asked Philip, 'Where shall we buy bread, that these may eat?' He was really testing Philip, 'for He Himself knew what He would do' (John 6:5–6). I realised as never before the implications for me of God's omniscience. Although we were called to apply to OMF at that time, He already knew what was going to happen to me physically, and He knew I was not fit to go to South-east Asia at that time. No wonder the directors at the OMF Headquarters in Singapore had had no leading from the Lord to accept our application.

At one stage of my protracted illness I developed major epileptic fits. This necessitated hospitalisation again and many tests to try to ascertain the cause. A mass was discovered on the right side of the fronto-temporal lobe of my brain. Further tests, including a carotid angiogram, were carried out. Although the doctors could not be sure of the nature of the mass, they were sure it was not cancerous. This relieved our minds, for both my father and his sister had died of a particularly malignant kind of brain cancer. I was discharged, and warned to continue indefinitely to take the anti-epileptic drugs that had been prescribed.

The monotony of my days was relieved by the occasional visits of patients to my bedroom. These patients were all women. They came to ask me to pray for their sick babies, their sick relatives or themselves. These visits grew more and more frequent and although I welcomed them they cost me much precious energy. On one occasion, even a ministers' fraternal was held in my bedroom. Eddie was concerned. He was planning to send me overseas to see if an orthopaedic surgeon he knew in north London could help me, because no doctor we had seen in South Africa had been able to do so. Unfortunately we did not have enough money for the flight overseas. Although there was an unwritten code in South Africa that doctors did not charge their colleagues in the medical profession, our finances had been severely strained by the need to pay for the weeks and months of hospitalisation in various hospitals. Because I was a doctor myself, I had always been allocated a single room wherever I had been admitted, and that meant the hospitalisation fees had been high. At that time we had no money saved on which we could draw.

Then Eddie had an idea that would kill two birds with one stone. While he stayed on at the mission hospital (and saved as much money as he could), he thought that I should spend some time at the holiday seaside cottage at Wilderness that we had bought years ago while we were still in private practice in Oudtshoorn. There I would have no demands made upon me, and I would become stronger. 'Manuku can go with you and look after you,' Eddie said. 'If you stay there with no one to bother you, you're bound to get stronger and be more able to stand the long flight to London.' Manuku was a gem of a home help, a Christian with a loving and caring spirit, and I readily agreed. Eddie booked her on the train for the 1,000 kilometre journey, but I could not manage such a long train trip, so for me he bought a plane ticket to George, the nearest town to our cottage overlooking a wide blue bay of rolling waves that washed the long, long beach of white sand.

At George airport I engaged a taxi to take me the short distance to the Wilderness. Soon we were there. The next thing I remember is standing before the door of the cottage, fitting my key into its lock. As I worked the key I suddenly heard, '*Dorothy*!' I looked round, but no one was there. I turned back to the door, only to hear once more, '*Dorothy*!'

I realised then that I had not actually heard a voice – I had 'heard' my name within myself, and I knew it was the Lord who had called me. I said, in my mind, *What do you want, Lord? We have no money; I am ill and unable to do anything for You.* And He replied, *You have plenty of time!* Of course this was true: although I had nothing else to give Him, I did have plenty of time. I decided then and there that I would give Him some of that time.

When Manuku arrived I told her what the Lord had said to me, and that I planned to set aside a time especially for Him in the morning and afternoon of each day. 'Will you join me in giving Him time?' I asked Manuku. 'I know that all the work and responsibility will be yours, here, because I can't help you.' She smiled warmly and said that she would be glad to join me and give time to the Lord. So, both morning and afternoon, we locked the door, unplugged the telephone and met in my bedroom where I lay on a mattress on the floor. Manuku was a Mosotho girl, and no Mosotho will ever pray before first singing a hymn, so we sang a verse from a hymn first and then took turns in reading from the Bible and praying.

Giving time to the Lord was a blessing to each of us. My own perception and understanding of God's greatness was steadily increased. As I woke each morning I would hobble to the bathroom, casting a glance outside the glassed-in doors that faced onto the beach. Every time I saw the expanse of white sand, washed clean of footmarks by the tides, it was as if I were seeing it on the day of creation, and I felt very near to God.

In the afternoon of the fourth day at the Wilderness – 3 March 1968 – I shut my eyes in preparation to pray, as it was my turn to do so, but I found I could not pray. I was convinced that the Lord's presence was with us in the room, and I was very conscious of my unworthy state, revealed before that holy presence. Even though I could not pray, I kept my eyes closed. I felt that if I opened them I would see a bright fiery light in the room and would be burned up. At last I remembered something I had learnt many years before in Sunday school and church. I remembered that because I had no righteousness of my own, I should pray in the righteousness of Jesus Christ, my Saviour, and that His righteousness would cover all my unworthiness. And so I prayed. I prayed in joy and praised Him for His wonderful love towards us. I was so absorbed by the miracle of His presence and His righteousness that it did not even enter my mind to pray for my healing.

The rest of that day was routine, with nothing especially memorable. But I shall never forget the next morning, when I woke up as usual with the light of dawn. On my way to and from the bathroom I felt strange – very strange. It was only as I entered my bedroom that I realised that, for the first time in three and a half years, I felt *well*!

I called excitedly to Manuku to tell her the good news. She came running and asked, '*Mme*[1] – are you feeling ill?' (She had been working for us for three years and had not known me before I had become an invalid.)

'No, Manuku – I'm *well*!' I answered her with a beaming face. Even my lanky, wasted body could not prevent her from hearing the joy in my voice. 'I'm well, and I'm hungry,' I went on.

---

[1] 'Mother', a term of respect from a younger woman to an older one.

'Hungry?' she asked, knowing that I had not been hungry since she had first come to work for us.

'Yes, I am,' I replied, 'and please help me bring the bed back into the room. While you get breakfast, I'll make up the bed. I'm never going to sleep on the floor again!'

From that day on I got up, dressed and went out to the beach of white sand to walk. After a week or so I was able to walk along the waves' edge for half a mile up and down. At that stage I decided it was time to telephone Eddie and tell him my wonderful news. He seemed to take my news very calmly and advised me to stay on at the Wilderness for another few weeks before returning home. What a disappointment that was. I had been picturing my homecoming, well at last, with Eddie and the children meeting me at Bloemfontein airport. However, such was the wonder that the Lord had done in me that without any objection I obediently agreed.

Three weeks later I flew home and Eddie came forward to meet me as I descended the steps of the plane.

'But you *are* well!' he exclaimed.

'I told you so!' I retorted. 'Didn't you believe me?'

And then he told me exactly what had run through his mind when he had heard me on the telephone. When he heard me saying I was walking up and down the seashore for a mile or so each day he found it incredible. He was convinced the mass in my brain had spread, and that I was now out of my mind. His thoughts had raced about, remembering that the children were about to return home for the school holidays. He had not wanted them to see their mother in this state of mental illness.

Back at home I made up my mind to continue to give

time to the Lord each morning and afternoon. Our domestic helps and gardener joined me in my bedroom for Bible reading and to kneel in prayer. One or two could not understand English so the gardener, Augustine, translated for them. During these times we were so absorbed in prayer that we were aware of nothing outside the room. One day Eddie returned home from the hospital to fetch some notes he needed for a lecture he was to give to the nurses. As he entered the house he was struck by the fact that it was apparently deserted. There was no sign of our gardener outside or of our cook in the kitchen. Wondering, he went down the passage to the bedroom to fetch his notes. He found me in a circle of others, all on our knees while one prayed aloud. Then, to his surprise, he saw a young postman also in the group, his bag and parcels beside him on the floor. Apparently he had knocked on the door but received no answer. He had heard of this habit of giving time to God twice daily, so made his way to the bedroom. We had been so lost to the outside world that we had not even heard him come in!

The experience of the blessing that came with giving time to the Lord has been ongoing. Having learnt to give Him that time, the habit has stayed with me for the rest of my life. The early morning hours spent with Him as I read His Word, meditate and pray are by far the most important of each day to me. They are absolutely indispensable.

> I love the LORD, because He has heard
> My voice and my supplications.
> Because He has inclined His ear to me,
> Therefore I will call upon Him as long as I live.
>
> (Psalm 116:1–2)

4

Another Chance

The crooked places shall be made straight
And the rough places smooth.

(Isaiah 40:4)

W e were surprised to receive a letter from Mr O.J. Sanders, the then General Director of the OMF, who had heard that I had been healed. He wrote praising the Lord with us and told us that if we still wanted to go to South-east Asia as missionaries, the OMF would welcome us gladly. He said that all I had to do was to see each doctor who had treated or operated on me and get the all-clear from them, as confirmation of my healing. I made appointments to see them and each one agreed that I was now healed – even though they could not understand it. Even the brain scan was repeated, and now showed no mass in my brain.

We duly reapplied to the OMF and were accepted. By this time our children were all of school-going age: David was ten, Anthony eight, Jennifer seven and Susan nearly six. In due time we left Thaba 'Nchu and went to stay in Cape

Town in the Andrew Murray Missionary Home belonging to OMF. While the children went to school I trained as an anaesthetist in Groote Schuur Hospital in order to be of more use in Manorom Hospital in Thailand when we finally got there. Eddie was a specialist general surgeon and I knew that there would always be a need for anaesthetics to be given.

During this time in Cape Town, Don Houliston, the South African Home Director of OMF told us that because Thailand's climate was not a healthy one for bringing up children, OMF had built Chefoo School in the cooler Cameron Highlands in Malaysia. He told us that our children would be required to go to school there. That meant they would be away from us for most of the year, returning home twice a year on seven-week-long holidays. 'Unfortunately,' he went on, 'your elder son, David, because he is already ten years old, will have to stay behind in South Africa. Chefoo is only a preparatory school, up to the age of eleven, and missionaries' children have to return to their home countries for their secondary education. If David went there too, he would have to leave again after only one year, and OMF HQ in Singapore do not believe that would be desirable. So will you please look for a suitable boarding school for him here in South Africa, and a couple among your friends who can act *in loco parentis* while you are in Thailand?'

This came as a shock to us. We were not happy to think how David, only ten years old, would be able to cope with the separation not only from his parents but also from his brother and two sisters. Nevertheless, we had to accept this situation. We found a Christian boys' boarding school in Port Elizabeth, about 500 miles east of Cape Town, where the rector was an old friend of ours. Stan and his wife Nance gladly offered to look after David for us as if he were their own son. (At that time we could not have imagined what a long-lasting and traumatic effect this separation would have on David, but more of that later.)

With regard to the three younger children, we were aware that the Malaysian government had passed a law that forbade any South African from entering that country. Eddie and I applied to Lesotho, asking for passports from that country, having worked for years among the Basotho people in Thaba 'Nchu. 'Yes, we would normally give you passports for Lesotho,' we were told, 'but in case you were forced to leave Thailand, we would not have the money available to pay for your return tickets.' Next, in desperation, we applied to the Canadian Trade Commission, thinking that they would be better off financially. But it was all in vain. We were stuck with our South African passports. This position caused us belatedly to turn to the Lord (how typical of us ordinary Christians!) to help us. When a well-wisher at an OMF prayer meeting commiserated with us because of this insuperable difficulty, saying that we would not be able to go out to Thailand after all, it was in faith that we replied, 'If God wants us to go to Thailand, He will arrange it in spite of any legislation.'

And that is exactly what happened. We applied for the visas, using the British consulate because Malaysia had no consular representation in South Africa at that time. After some weeks Eddie was summoned to the consulate. When he entered the reception area he found several people already waiting for attention. Most were standing, while an elderly, white-haired man was sitting, looking at a copy of the *London Illustrated News*. Suddenly a stentorian voice broke into the soft hum of conversation: 'Will you please all stand in line and wait your turn!' Every face looked up at the large, officious woman behind the counter. 'And that man sitting over there – will you please stand up and join the queue?' There was a general shuffle and gradually an orderly queue formed. The rather decrepit old man slowly straightened his back and obeyed the dictatorial voice, standing at the back of the line. Eddie took his place behind the elderly man and waited his turn.

When Eddie finally reached the counter, the embassy official looked up at his face and then down again at the children's passports that she had before her. She stamped each one with the British consulate stamp for a visa. Then she took up her pen to write in the details that were required.

Suddenly she sighed and shook her head, saying in a tiny voice, 'I *can't* go on!'

Eddie looked at her in surprise. 'Are you ill?' he asked.

'No, Dr Rose. You may not know, but permission for the children's visas came through a little while ago. Now I knew that this would be against the law that forbids any South African, man, woman or child, to set foot in Malaysia. You see, I worked in the British consulate in Malaysia for several years some time ago. So I sent a cable to them, saying that the permission that had been granted was entirely against their law, as the children had South African passports, not British ones. But a cable came back from Malaysia with just two words: "Visas confirmed!"' She shook her head slightly in incredulity. 'Do you know the *Tunku*, the ruler of Malaysia?'

'No,' replied Eddie simply. 'I know Someone much higher. And He has just shown me that He can override any man-made law.'

The confused lady then asked Eddie whether the OMF still had prayer meetings in Singapore every Friday. 'I used to visit a friend of mine in Singapore sometimes when I was on holiday, and she took me with her to a few of the OMF prayer meetings,' she explained in reply to his questioning look.

Eventually, she completed the visas stamped in the children's passports and Eddie returned to the OMF missionary home with the wonderful news that now there was nothing more to delay us.

5

On the Way

How long will your journey be?
(Nehemiah 2:6)

We happily prepared for the journey to Thailand,
having decided to take David with us as well as
the three younger children. He would stay
with us for three weeks so he could see for himself where
we would be living and then fly back to South Africa. In
early 1969 passenger ships still plied the ocean, so Eddie
booked us on a ship bound for Singapore. At the time that
OMF wanted us there, there was only one vessel bound for
South-east Asia – the SS *Cathay*, a P & O liner.

In those days the OMF had a policy that new missionaries
should bear the cost of their outward-bound voyage. The
provision of sufficient funds was regarded as a confirmation
of God's call. We therefore had to pay for the fares for a family of six. However, my protracted illness had drained us of
all our savings. Where was the necessary money going to
come from? Then Eddie remembered something. 'Dossie,
do you remember the plot of land near the sea at Little Brak

River we bought years ago, so we could build a holiday home there one day? We can sell that. We don't need it any more; we're going to be missionaries!'

And so we decided to sell that prime land on the seafront. Eddie received an offer for the land by long-distance telephone. When asked to name his price, Eddie worked out a fair price in his estimation and told the potential buyer. Promptly, the man accepted the price and this was agreed on verbally. Because Eddie has always been ultra-careful, he drove to Little Brak River and asked the owners of neighbouring plots the going price for their land. To his astonishment, the price of these plots had risen by 300 per cent since we had bought our land. He came home, fully intending to telephone the buyer and tell him he had made a mistake in naming the price. But when we thought it through and prayed over it, the thought came that we should abide by Jesus' teaching, 'Let your "Yes" be "Yes," and your "No," "No"' (Matthew 5:37). The agreement to sell was not yet in writing, so we could still have altered the price, particularly as the buyer lived nearby and had known the rocketing value of land in that area when he had first telephoned. Nevertheless, we decided to let our 'Yes' be 'Yes' and agreed to let the sale go through at the original price. To our amazement, the price realised by the sale was exactly enough to pay for the fares of all six of us and also for David's return airfare.

Before we left for the East it had been arranged that the veteran missionary of the China Inland Mission, Hayden Mellsopp, should accompany us on a deputation tour round South Africa. We left the children in the good hands of Don and Sylvia Houliston and off we went in the mission's car.

We had meetings at a number of towns along the route laid out for us and were becoming accustomed to telling how God had called us to become missionaries and how He had opened the way for us to go in spite of difficulties. One morning Eddie received a letter with the OMF logo on the envelope. Curiously, he opened it. His face fell in dismay as he saw it was an account for our empty room at the Andrew Murray House for the eight weeks we were to be away. 'I don't understand,' he said. 'How can this be? We aren't even occupying the room! And in any case we're already working for OMF doing this deputation.' He wanted to go immediately to tell Hayden about this new development, which he considered most unfair. Being an extremely orderly and responsible man, Eddie had seen that all accounts had been prepaid and that we owed nothing. All we had left had been spent on the tickets for the *Cathay*. So how could we pay this account for an unoccupied room?

I dissuaded Eddie from rushing off to tell Hayden and he agreed to wait until he was calmer. And so we continued with the deputation tour. One day, not very long after the receipt of the account, Hayden was driving us to the venue for the next meeting when Eddie started to tell him what had happened. He sat forward on the edge of the back seat and his words simply spilled out. I held my breath. What would Hayden say and how would he advise us? Eddie and I were both taken aback by his immediate, gentle response. 'Isn't the Lord good to you?' he replied. 'Now you have an opportunity to trust Him for what you need even *before* you go to the East!'

Dumbfounded, Eddie sank back in his seat. With one gentle sentence, this man of God had whipped away our smouldering resentment and taught us a lesson in faith that we have never forgotten. Many people at the deputation meetings had already donated money towards the Lord's work through the Overseas Missionary Fellowship. But after this conversation, for the next two weeks, some people came to give us money 'towards unexpected expenses'. (They had no means of knowing that an unexpected expense had indeed turned up.) Even more significant was the fact that after the amount we owed for the room had been given – with a few rands over – these specific donations simply stopped. This miraculous supply of our unexpected need made us realise we could trust in the Lord absolutely and be anxious for nothing.

At last the time came for us to board the *Cathay*. The voyage took three weeks. It was uneventful, the sea was calm and the weather lovely. We played deck games and got to know fellow passengers. The highlight for the children was, I think, the fancy dress party. They came clamouring for me to make costumes for them. *Costumes for all four?* I thought in panic. *For a few days' time? How on earth can I even think of making four costumes with only a couple of rolls of crêpe paper?* I had to reply, so I played for time and said I would think about it. In fact, I was at my wits' end. With no sewing machine or adequate materials available, my mind raced without getting anywhere. Then a thought struck me. Not many months previously Professor Christian Barnard had pioneered the world's first heart transplant. Surely I could make something of that.

I started eagerly to bring my idea to life. Elaborate costumes were impossible, so I decided to use everyday articles already in the cabin. I took some sheets and pillowslips from the bunks, commandeered the ladder to the top bunk in the children's cabin, and borrowed two items from the ship's doctor. David, the eldest, was to be Professor Barnard. I draped him in a sheet instead of a white coat. Anthony, also in a white sheet, was the anaesthetist. Jennifer was the nurse and Susan, lying on the lightweight ladder for the upper berth, was the patient. The three pillowslips I used to make theatre caps. To make it clear to all that Anthony was the anaesthetist, I let him have an empty plastic talcum powder container that was in a concertina-like shape. As he walked beside the 'stretcher' he squashed the container repeatedly till it rose again, just like the rebreathing bag of an anaesthetic machine. Susan lay with her eyes closed while Jennifer and David carried the makeshift stretcher. Next to Susan lay a kidney dish half full of tomato sauce. All eyes in the audience were on David, who carried artery forceps holding a heart-shaped piece of cardboard that was dripping great red drops of tomato sauce into the kidney dish. It was fortunate no one was squeamish. In fact the tableau was a great success and the children received first prize!

The days and weeks passed, broken only by a few short stops. At the Seychelles we anchored near the main island of Mahé for a few days and were taken ashore by launch in relays. The crystal-clear water around us revealed shoals of brightly coloured small fish in the surrounding sea. The island smelled of spices and reminded me of the time my mother had taken us as children to the island of Zanzibar. The difference was that in Zanzibar the smell was of cloves, whereas here it was a sweet scent of cinnamon. Later, as we were driven round the island, our driver pointed out the great shrubs that lined the narrow roads. 'These are the cinnamon trees,' he said. 'They are the best source of income for us poor islanders.' We rounded the final bend before reaching the landing stage once more and came across a fairy-tale scene – a bay of soft wavelets lapping gently at a curving beach of white sand that almost hurt our eyes as it reflected the brilliant sunlight. Palm trees lining the bay moved slightly with the mild breeze that cooled our hot faces. Our driver suggested that we stop for a while to enjoy the scene. The children poured out of the old car in the wink of an eye and Eddie and I followed a little more sedately, to take off our sandals, cross the hot white sand to the water's edge and paddle in the lukewarm sea. The pause was refreshing in spite of the inescapable heat and humidity.

The next stop was in Bombay. Again we were invited to go ashore, although a starker contrast with the Seychelles could hardly be imagined. The sea across which we were taken in a launch was choppy and a dirty grey-green colour. Once ashore we took a pedicab to see round the city. My lasting impression is one of dirt – dirty buildings and dirty streets, with litter in every corner. Our driver pointed out a large building that he said was a maternity hospital. Eddie and I were interested, of course, but we shuddered when we saw the grime of the unpainted building and its surroundings. It was bad enough to know that this building was a medical establishment – so much worse that it was a *maternity* hospital.

It was while we were in Bombay that Indian crowds boarded the ship, some to offer things for sale and others solely to beg. We were surprised to see that two women

passengers in their sixties, who had up to that time refused
to have anything to do with people of another race, had an
abrupt change of heart at the sight of the young Hindu children and babies who accompanied the vendors. For the first
two weeks these women had been insular in their views
and wary of the other passengers: they had not even dared
to greet the High Commissioner of Ceylon, Sir Rajapakse,
and his elegant wife. These ladies had never had any social
contact with people of dark complexions and were reluc-
tant to do so now. Unexpectedly, however, the sight of the
brown-skinned babies and children who now thronged the
deck won their hearts and we were amazed to see these
rather aloof women clasping babies to their breasts and
rocking them to sleep. It had taken just a few weeks to
widen their horizon after decades of prejudice.

When the ship called in at Port Swettenham in Malaysia
and passengers were invited to go ashore, we could not risk
leaving the ship with the rest. We learned later from Mr
Arnold Lea, the Overseas Director of OMF, that if we had
gone, such a visit would have used up the precious visas for
the children and they would not have been allowed to enter
Malaysia again in order to attend Chefoo School.

At last we sighted numerous small islands all around us.
We realised that we were nearing the island state of Singapore, where we would disembark. The intensely hot,
humid air hung heavily about us, giving us our first experience of what we would have to deal with living in the
sweaty heat of South-east Asia.

The OMF Mission Home in Singapore was set in pleasant
surroundings opposite a park filled with lush green grass,
exotic tropical flowers and varieties of palms. The three

younger children cheerfully went off by train to the OMF's school in Malaysia, which had been called Chefoo after a school in China run by the China Inland Mission many years ago. They were in the care of Audrey Jackson, a secretary in the office, who was British and had no difficulty travelling in and out of Malaysia. Eddie, David and I stayed in the mission home for the weekend. It was exciting being there. The streets were crowded with cars and motorbikes and on the pavements and in the shops were people in different costumes, according to their nationality and culture. Turbaned Sikhs rubbed shoulders with men in Malay dress, while women in their colourful saris did their shopping.

One day Beryl Eksteen, a fellow South African and a missionary with OMF of some years, took us to an open-air eating place off the famous Orchard Road, where wobbly tables surrounded by stools dotted an open square. Huge flat umbrellas shielded customers from the fierce sun. As we looked about us at the milling crowds, Beryl went to one of the many stalls to order some food for each of us. 'You won't know what to order here,' she said, 'and every bowl of food here costs exactly the same – one US dollar.' She came back with bowls heaped with noodles in sauce and our noses twitched with the tantalising smell and our mouths watered in anticipation. We started eating gingerly, but soon were heaping our spoons eagerly.

After a few minutes I looked up from my bowl and asked, 'Beryl, why is it that most of the noodles are soft but every now and again one is tough?'

'The tougher ones are squid,' she explained.

'*Squid!*' I froze, my spoon in mid-air.

My appetite suddenly disappeared. I had never eaten

such a thing before. The romantic East was no longer romantic. Was this the first hurdle to be faced in my missionary career? I forced down the piece of squid that was in my mouth and prayed at the same time that it would stay down.

Before we knew it, the two days were over and we were on our way to the Singapore docks, where we boarded a Polish cargo vessel, the *Kapitan Kosco*, bound for Bangkok. We three were to be the only passengers. As we boarded the vessel we noticed it was so heavily laden that the gangway on which we were walking was horizontal instead of sloping upwards as is normally the case. Because the holds were already overfilled, large carboys were packed closely side by side, filling the forecastle. As the voyage progressed we saw sailors hosing these carboys down with seawater in the hottest part of each day. Only one man of the crew, the ship's doctor, could speak English, heavily accented though it was. When we asked him about this practice he calmly told us that the carboys contained concentrated hydrochloric acid and that they were hosed down to try to prevent any possibility of spontaneous combustion. His explanation did nothing to quell our uneasiness, though familiarity with the procedure gradually lulled us into acceptance.

We were served a lot of meals on board the *Kapitan Kosco*: five full meals each day as well as tea and coffee with snacks in between the meals. We found to our surprise that drinking water was both precious and scarce. Instead, wine was freely available at each meal. It is not every missionary who has only wine to drink on the way to the mission field! Finding enough water for ten-year-old David to drink was difficult. In spite of the enervating heat only one bottle of soda water was supplied in each cabin, and that had to last for 24 hours. When we asked for more soda water we were told there was none to spare.

After four days we reached the Chao Phrya river delta and could feast our eyes on the jungle greens of Thailand, so near at last. A pilot boarded us there and guided the ship slowly into the narrow channel at the mouth of the delta. We were standing on deck when an outgoing ship passed ours and were horrified to see that only two feet of churned-up white water separated us from the 8,000-ton vessel. We had undoubtedly arrived in the nonchalant East. When we reached the docks of outer Bangkok and could see the figures of people awaiting the vessel on the quay, the ship unexpectedly came to a halt. 'But we're still in the middle of the river!' I exclaimed, dumbfounded. Eddie soon came to us with the reason for the lack of further progress. The ship was so overladen and low in the water that it could not navigate the shallower parts of the river. 'How will we ever be able to get ashore?' I did not want to stay in the middle of the river, and was eager to see the land where we were to work. I need not have been agitated, as shortly the innovative Thai stevedores on the bank organised large floating cranes that could reach into our ship and lift off quantities of cargo from the vessel. Gradually the ship rose in the water, until it was able at last to anchor nearer the dock. It did not seem to matter to the Thai that the ship was still 15 feet from the quayside. A simple Heath-Robinson-type gangway was quickly assembled and then extended to the ship.

We hurriedly got all our possessions together. We wanted to be ready to leave as soon as we had permission from the immigration officials who boarded the ship immediately after it docked. But what a let-down! The OMF office had supplied us with visas for Thailand, but somehow had made the mistake of getting only tourist visas. Not only was our own luggage more than most tourists had, but we had also been saddled with large packages of medical and laboratory equipment for Manorom Hospital – hundreds of surgical gloves, microscopes and the like. We had not been aware of these additions to our own luggage. The immigration official was adamant. We could leave the ship only if we carried the bare essentials with us. We could not take the rest of our luggage. Nor could we even take our camera. We left the locked suitcases in our cabin and the ship's captain locked the cabin door in front of us and pocketed the key. In great expectancy (and some trepidation) we filed down the gangway to the quayside, where the OMF Director for Thailand was waiting patiently to greet us. Our new life in the tropics of South-east Asia was about to begin.

6

Asia at Last!

I have showed thee new things.
(Isaiah 48:6 KJV)

As we left the *Kapitan Kosco* to walk down the gangway the hot and humid air felt like a wall before
us. We had not noticed the intensity of the heat or
the 'solidity' of the humid air while we were still on board,
as the movement of the ship had brought a little breeze to
us, which disappeared as soon as the ship was still. We did
not know then that April is always the hottest month of the
year in Thailand. Later we learned that the three seasons of
the year there were the hot season, the hotter season and
the hottest season. The impending approach of the annual
monsoon increased the normal humidity. To us newcomers
the heat was unbearable. I said as much to Isaac Scott, the
OMF Thailand Director. 'It's not so bad today,' was his reply,
'there's a slight breeze.' (The breeze was indeed slight – we
had not even been aware of it.)

The driver of the mission car took us carefully through
busy traffic, past a very smelly canal in the centre of

Sathorn Road's dual carriageway and on to the mission home in Pan Road. Immediately on entering the building we were brought welcome glasses of iced water. Never had plain water tasted so delicious! Then we were shown to our room. The windows were shaded and the beds looked welcoming. Before starting to unpack the little we had been allowed to take with us, I could not resist sitting down on the bed. I had hardly sat down when I sprang up again as if I had been stung. I had never come across a bed so hard. On investigation I found the mattress was extremely thin, with kapok stuffing. When I asked about this later, we were told that it was the coolest type of mattress to sleep on in Thailand's heat. At first disbelieving, I finally became resigned to the thin kapok mattress because I found that its hardness left no space for hot pockets of air and so it really was cooler than the more comfortable sprung mattress I had enjoyed in South Africa.

We had landed on a Friday afternoon. The main customs/immigrations office had already closed when we finally reached land. Because of this, it had not been possible to sort out the contretemps caused by our arrival with only tourist visas plus the mountain of luggage for Manorom Hospital that OMF had sent with us. An official on the dock told us that, because of the weekend to come and the public holiday on Monday, nothing could be done until the next Tuesday. The Union Language School's new term was due to start that day, so Isaac Scott decided I should attend the language school while Eddie would return to the docks.

On Tuesday, therefore, Eddie returned to the docks accompanied by Prasert, a smiling interpreter from the

OMF office. Together they spent almost the entire day talking back and forth with officials. Eventually they paid a fine of 6,000 baht, and the luggage was released. To Eddie's horror, when he opened our large suitcase, the camera had simply disappeared. It was our first encounter with the incredible ingenuity of the Thai when it came to stealing. We were to get to know it well, though this first experience was a shock indeed.

At the language school I joined a beginners' class of young missionaries together with a couple of Westerners who needed to learn Thai for business purposes. The women teachers were very well groomed and, for the most part, wore silk dresses. Three of the four hours of that day's classes were spent on listening and learning to recognise the five tones that are an integral part of the Thai language. By the time we left the school to begin the long walk home I was exhausted. When I saw Eddie after his return from the docks he looked as bedraggled as I felt. We were both so tired that we slept that night on the hard beds without even being conscious of any discomfort.

The next day Eddie accompanied me to the language school. The teacher stood in front of the class, her words dropping into the silence like a bombshell: 'Today we start with a test.' Numbed with shock, Eddie could not contemplate starting his first day with a test. Humbly he raised his hand. He did not need to speak, for like a wraith, the silken shape of *Khruu*[1] Saowan, the assistant head teacher, was beside him in an instant. 'Dr Rose,' she murmured, 'of course you need to catch up.' (*Catch up?* he thought in desperation.

---

[1] 'Teacher' (in a school).

Already?) 'Come, follow me,' she went on, moving towards the door. Eddie followed her obediently and found himself in another room, empty except for two chairs facing each other. In one chair sat a stunningly beautiful young woman, dressed in dazzling white silk. The other chair was empty. *Khruu* Saowan glided back through the door.

'Please sit down,' said the vision in a soft voice, smiling winningly. 'My name is *Khruu* Suchitraa, and I will be teaching you so that you can catch up with the rest of your class.' Eddie gingerly lowered himself into the chair opposite Suchitraa. 'Nearer, please,' she said, and again repeated the request for him to draw his chair nearer hers. Soon their knees were almost touching. 'Now, watch my lips as I speak,' she said. 'Watch my lips.' And Eddie had an almost irresistible urge to burst into laughter. 'What is funny?' inquired Suchitraa innocently. Eddie pulled himself together and started to concentrate on the sounds and tones she uttered until he could identify and recognise the five different tones used in the Thai language. The next day he rejoined the class, but only after the teacher had rejected his plaintive comment that he thought he needed more personal tuition.

After a week in the mission home we moved to an old wooden two-storey house a few miles away. Isaac Scott had decided to rent this house for us as it was very near to the language school we would be attending. It was simply unfortunate that this language school had moved in the meantime to a location a couple of miles beyond the mission home! I will always remember this house for the lessons I learned about housekeeping in Thailand while we were living in it.

First, and most important, we learned that no one ever entered a home without first removing shoes or sandals and leaving them outside the door. Because of this, every floor in the house had to be washed each day so that people's bare feet would not become dirty. I do not think I will ever forget the hours I spent each day on my knees washing those old teak floors, the perspiration from my face and arms running down to join the water in the bucket. It would not have been so bad except for the incredible heat. The second lesson I learned was from our landlady, who lived in a small wooden house in the same compound. 'When you buy a chicken from the market,' she warned me, 'make sure it is still alive. If it is already dead you won't be able to tell what it died from!' The third lesson was in the field of housekeeping economics. I had asked Eddie to go to the market nearby to buy some bean sprouts for the stir-fry I wanted to make for our lunch. He took a few baht with him and walked to the market. About 15 minutes later he returned, bearing two huge sacks filled to the brim with bean sprouts, one under each arm. Answering my inquiring look, he said, 'Well, I asked the vendor for bean sprouts and gave her a baht – and she gave me her entire stock!' We certainly had not realised how cheaply one could live in this land. At that time 20 baht was equivalent to one US dollar.

Another lesson concerned the state of the meat available from the market. One day I set out to buy some meat. The market was not far away and soon I joined in the hubbub and bustle of housewives looking for bargains. Stalls were close together, with narrow pathways between them. A peculiar smell – a bit fishy, garlicky and just plain dirty – met me as I penetrated the first layer of stalls. Tin buckets lay to the side of the pathway, with live catfish moving lazily in the water they contained. Large live crabs hung in festoons – I had to be careful to avoid their claws as I picked my way round the puddles of grimy water that lay in my path. I looked about me everywhere, but could not see a meat stall. In my halting Thai I asked a vendor of strange-looking vegetables where I could buy meat. 'There,' she pointed, waving an arm. Obediently I walked on for a few minutes in the direction she had indicated, but was still unable to find the meat stalls. I chose a friendly looking woman in charge of a stall with ducks and chickens hanging in front, and asked her where I should go. 'There!' she said and flung out her arm towards a stall only a few feet away. Looking in that direction, I saw black clouds of buzzing flies, disturbed by her theatrical gesture, rising up from the stall and revealing the slabs of meat they had been covering.

David's three weeks in Thailand came to an end too soon. It was with heavy hearts that we took him to the international airport, Don Muang, and saw him off. My last sight of him was from the observation level, high above the ground, as he walked next to one of the hostesses. He had been given all the passengers' passports to hold and he walked proudly and steadily to the plane. My tears flowed and I could not stop weeping in spite of Eddie's arms about me. As the chartered Boeing 707 stood on the tarmac I could not help seeing that the glint of the sun revealed numerous bumps and dents in the body of the aircraft – in fact, it looked as if it had been used as practice by a panel-beater. How could I ever trust it to take our son so far away? I felt as if David would never reach South Africa.

After David's plane had taken off we descended from the

roof of the airport building to the ground level. In front of us as we stepped off the final stair was a barber-cum-hairdressing salon. A few days earlier, Eddie had mentioned that he needed a haircut badly as he had not had one since he left South Africa, but he was very nervous about places in Bangkok. He could not forget stories he had heard about massage parlours in Thailand masquerading as barbers. 'Why don't I go in here for a haircut?' he said now. 'The airport ought to be a safe place for me to go. You can wait outside for me – I shouldn't be long.' I watched him go through the entrance of the salon and then wandered about, looking at the sights that were still fascinating to me as we had not been in Thailand all that long.

Twenty minutes later Eddie emerged from the salon. I gaped – I could not take my eyes from his face, which was as white as a sheet. 'What's happened?' I asked him solicitously.

'Let's find somewhere we can sit down and I'll tell you,' he murmured weakly. We found a bench nearby and he told me all that had happened.

From the moment he had entered the salon he was shocked to find it was decorated in pink – pink seats, pink and gold round the mirrors, pink capes for the clients and pink dresses like saris for the attendants. *What kind of place is this, then?* he thought nervously, but stoically allowed himself to be guided to a seat and then endured the humiliation of having a pink cape arranged round his shoulders. While he was waiting for someone to attend to him, he watched the comings and goings behind him reflected in the mirror. Gradually he became aware of a feminine figure in pink gliding in his direction. When she was within touching distance she stopped beside him on his left. She stretched out her right arm towards him until her hand was touching his thigh. Eddie's body grew rigid. *What does she want?* His thoughts raced madly. *If she goes any higher, I'm out of here!* His limbs tensed, ready for immediate action. Then her hand began to move, gently but inexorably upwards.

He was on the point of erupting from his seat and escaping from this den of iniquity when the searching hand found his own hand, as it rested on his thigh. 'Manicure?' came the gentle voice.

'Only a haircut, please!' came Eddie's strangled reply. No wonder he was so ashen when he came out of the salon.

One hot, hot afternoon not long after we had settled into the old house, Isaac Scott and his wife Eileen collected us to walk to the busy shopping centre half a mile away. They wanted to show us a shop where goods were sold more cheaply than in others. As we walked along in the heat and dense humidity, we wilted and walked more and more slowly. Isaac used this time to tell us not to waste our money on buying cans or bottles of cool drinks. 'You can make your own cool drinks,' he said. 'Just boil water and sugar together to make a syrup, add a drop of food colouring, and then flavour it with some essence. You must remember to put in a little bit of citric acid, or it will be too sweet and bland. Your home-made cool drinks will be much cheaper and just as refreshing.' We took all this in, nodding at his wise advice. At last we reached the shop we were going to and found it a shadowed place, cooled by a large overhead fan. After introductions and an initial order of groceries we turned to start the walk home. At the crossroads just before our house, the Scotts turned right towards their own home. No sooner were they out of sight than, with a quick glance of mutual understanding at each other, Eddie and I made a beeline for the rickety shop on the corner and bought two bottles of Coca-Cola. We drank with pleasure as the cool liquid relieved our parched throats. The extreme heat and humidity had so dehydrated us that we felt we could not possibly have waited any longer. (Later on, however, when we were settled, I obediently made bottles of concentrated syrup.)

The time we spent in the old wooden house was especially memorable for Eddie. At night he found he could not possibly sleep in pyjamas because of the heat. (We had not realised that we should have bought a fan to help make living in Bangkok bearable in that season.) He came from the bathroom dripping wet and lay as he was on top of his kapok mattress and sweated. Every two or three hours, when the heat had dried his body, he was obliged to get up and go to the bathroom again. The bathroom was like no other we had known. It was almost completely empty but for a large Ali Baba jar filled with water with a plastic dipper floating on the surface. At the other end of the same room was a flat porcelain Thai toilet only a few inches higher than the floor. This room was 'showerproof' as, no matter how much water one splashed around during one's ablutions, it did not matter. Eddie went to the Ali Baba jar and threw dipper after dipper of the lukewarm water over his sweating body. When he was dripping wet he returned, still naked, and lay on top of his bed, where he dozed fitfully until the heat had dried his body again. This pattern of behaviour he repeated night after night. One evening he felt so desperate that he said, 'Dorothy, I think this place is unbearable. I can't *stand* the heat!' But I replied philosophically,

'Well, Eddie, 60 million Thai live here – and if they can, so can we.' And so we stuck it out somehow.

After we had been living there for some weeks I became accustomed to sweeping and washing the wooden floors both upstairs and downstairs every day, without respite from the enervating and incredible heat. One day I managed to finish the unpacking, hang a picture or two and arrange little ornaments to make the place feel like home. A few days later we had an urgent message from Mission HQ telling us that because we had been given incorrect visas we would have to return to Singapore – and that we had only 24 hours in which to pack up all our belongings again. So out came our suitcases and into them we packed all our personal possessions once more. Our boxes of linen and household goods were stored at the mission home. This time, however, we were given plane tickets and the flight to Singapore took only a few hours instead of the four days it had taken to travel by sea.

One of the OMF directors based in Singapore met us at the airport and drove us to a housing estate where he showed us a townhouse that was for our use. We looked at the rooms and the few pieces of essential furniture that were in them. I was worried. *How are we going to live here without bed linen, towels, crockery or cutlery?* A knock at the door cut short my doubts and our very first visitors, Mr and Mrs Norman MacIntosh, appeared, smiling warmly as they welcomed us. They had been working as missionaries based in Singapore for years. After introducing themselves, they returned to their vehicle to gather up all the items they had borrowed from other missionaries on our behalf. What a relief it was to see them! We would not have known what to do or whom to ask, but the MacIntoshes were friends with all the other OMF missionaries in Singapore and had known just what we would need. They brought enough for five, because it would soon be time for the next Chefoo vacation and the three children would be joining us in the townhouse.

It was steamy and hot in Singapore – but not quite as bad as in Thailand, thank goodness. The house had uncarpeted cement floors and ceiling fans in each room, and these things helped us manage. A young man came twice weekly on a motorcycle to deliver groceries and to take a new order. One day, as he stood outside the open kitchen door, he looked inside with a puzzled expression and said, 'Why have you nothing on the floors of your house? Everywhere else I go there are carpets or linoleum.' He did not know that we were glad the floors were bare. Whether or not they helped the house stay cool, I do not know. Nonetheless, the feel of them under our bare feet certainly gave the *impression* of coolness.

At the end of our second week in Singapore we were told of the children's imminent arrival. We took a pedicab to the railway station to meet them. Soon the train puffed into the station. We craned our necks to look for our three children between the crowds waiting on the platform. Suddenly a little girl with golden plaits came rushing towards us. It was Susan. Only six years old, she somehow looked more self-assured now, even though she had been away for only six weeks. With a brand-new American accent and vocabulary that she had picked up even during this short time away from us, she said, 'Hi, Ma – I guess I left my sweater on the train!'

While we were in Singapore we attended the orientation course for missionary candidates in another part of the city. We had a very basic introduction to the Thai language, given by a slightly built Thai woman who was devastated by her unhappy marriage. Most of what we learned concerned Eastern and Thai culture. One day we had a lecture by an influential Chinese businessman on the historical background and socio-economic conditions found in East Asian countries. He told us that in his opinion the East was not much of a buyer's market for the missionary to 'sell' Christianity. His talk shook us out of our complacency and made us rethink our Western ideas rather than trying simply to import them to the East.

One afternoon we were in the city centre with the children, starting to cross a street. Suddenly the roar of an approaching motorcycle startled us with its rapid crescendo as it came racing down the street. The rider did not slow down at all, although eight-year-old Jennifer was in his path and was hurled to the tarmac. He was soon out of sight. We gathered round Jennifer's prostrate form in trepidation. Eddie picked her up gently and carried her to a nearby shop where she could lie down. The sympathetic owner provided a chair and offered me a cup of tea. Eventually we were able to return home. We knew she would have better care at home with us than anywhere else. Jennifer remained unconscious, so Eddie and I took turns in keeping vigil over her all through the night. Dreadful thoughts of possible permanent brain damage kept recurring, but the solace and strengthening that came from heartfelt prayer kept us at peace in spite of these fears.

The next morning Jenny opened her eyes and seemed

none the worse for her devastating experience. The Singapore police were informed and wanted us to make a charge against the motorcyclist, but we did not do so because the OMF Field Director, Arnold Lea, had advised us not to become involved in a case of this sort. He said that such a case would inevitably delay our return to Thailand, and reminded us that our goal was Thailand, not Singapore. The children returned to Chefoo School in due course, and after three more months in Singapore we flew back to Thailand.

7

Language School Beginnings

> . . . people of unfamiliar speech and of hard language.
>
> (Ezekiel 3:6)

On our return to Bangkok we expected to encounter once more the fierce heat we had experienced in April, so we were pleasantly surprised as we emerged from the plane to find the weather much more bearable this time. We were met at the airport and taken on the Asian Highway until we entered the bustling streets of the huge, sprawling city. When we drove along Sathorn Road we recoiled from the reek of the foul-smelling, sludgy canal that ran alongside it. This discomfort was short-lived, thankfully, as we soon turned off into a narrower road and parked in front of a large building surrounded by grass and shrubs. This was Study House, where we would be staying with other new missionary candidates while we learned the Thai language.

Most of the candidates were single women and were housed in the main building. The upper floors had been altered to accommodate them in pairs. This year there were only two married couples. We found that our living quarters were in fact half of a long garage. Ulrich and Adele Juzi, a Swiss-German couple, were to live in the other half with their two small boys. A hastily erected wooden structure between our large rooms had been fitted with toilets and showers, and this was remarkably effective in providing some measure of privacy for both families. When our three children came from Chefoo on holiday they shared our room with us. To enable them to sleep when Eddie and I had a light on at night, we bought some metres of patterned blue cotton material that Adele hemmed for me to make a curtain room-divider.

We were at the language school from 8 o'clock until noon each morning and were required to study at home for four hours each afternoon. In the grounds of Study House was a separate long building that housed a language laboratory, which we could make use of whenever we liked. The fact that it was air-conditioned made it very attractive to us and encouraged us to study! We revelled in the fact that the language school itself was also air-conditioned. While we were in classes we could forget Bangkok's intense heat. At 7.30 a.m., when we walked the two miles to the school, it was early enough for the heat to be bearable. However, as the hands of our watches inevitably drew near to noon each day, our hearts sank at the prospect of walking back home in the glaring sunlight, sweltering heat and unbearably high humidity. The long walk seemed interminable. We trudged doggedly along the hot, dirty streets and twisting, narrow lanes of Bangkok. The pavements were uneven with ridges due to subsidence and gaps left by previous floods. The lanes were made narrower by the high walls surrounding properties on either side. Their huge gates were always shut. Inserted into a gate would be a small locked door for pedestrians. Traffic roared incessantly along the streets and made conversation impossible. We sweated profusely. I would borrow Eddie's large handkerchief to mop my face, arms and legs as we walked. We sighed as we wished we could afford the few baht for one of the three-wheeled motorbike taxis.

Even as the months passed and the monsoon season started for Central Thailand, we kept doggedly walking. In the mornings a heavy shower with huge drops of rain would often drench us so that we would arrive at the language school dripping from head to toe. In the classrooms, thanks to the lowered humidity brought about by the air-conditioners, it was not long before we were dry again. We never needed to use a towel. In the afternoons it was common to be soaked again as we walked back to Study House through ankle-deep puddles that appeared in a matter of minutes along the pavements. We women kept on our sandals to protect our feet from sharp objects under the water, but, especially when the water was deeper, Eddie took off his shoes and socks and rolled up his trousers, while I simply lifted my skirt above my knees. As time passed, we became accustomed to these sudden soakings and learned to ignore them.

The Thai language was not like any other language we knew. In South Africa we had been brought up to be bilingual, as it was a government requirement that all citizens should be proficient in English and Afrikaans. We had already picked up a fair amount of other languages – Southern

Sotho, Tswana, and a smattering of Italian and Xhosa, but the Thai language was quite different from any of these. It involved no clicks like some of the African languages, thankfully, but we were horrified to find that we were to learn a language that had five different tones, as well as 28 vowels and 52 consonants. Each consonant is named – even primary schoolchildren in Thailand know all the names – and I suppose that is because there are several consonants that sound the same. For instance, 't' can be written in seven different ways, a suitable consonant being chosen for its exact instructions to the reader as to tone and production. There are four different consonants for 'p' and four for 's'. When the final letter of a word is 's' it is pronounced as 't'. In Thai writing no capitals are ever used and there are no breaks for paragraphs. There are no punctuation marks at all, either. Words are not separated by spaces, but run together one after the other.

Because the language has five tones, a change in the intonation of a word will change the meaning of that word completely. Once, before taking a train upcountry, Eddie stood in a queue at the station to purchase a ticket. When he asked for a ticket, the official stared at him blankly. Eddie tried again, but met with the same result. Baffled, he waited a moment, wondering what he should do, when a Thai man behind him in the queue spoke up and told the official that Eddie wanted a *ticket* and not what he had apparently asked for – a *body*! Another word very easy to mispronounce, simply because of slightly different tones, was the word for a dress. If one went into a shop to ask to see a dress, it was extremely easy to find oneself asking for a tiger by mistake.

In our class at language school that first year, Eddie was the only man. The Thai consider a man far more important than a woman and Eddie always had the doubtful honour of being the first to be asked to read or answer a question. Gradually the use of English by our teachers became less and less, until all the teaching was given in Thai, and we had to respond to questions in Thai too.

We found that our language learning did not progress steadily. At times we would be buoyed up by small achievements, while at other times we would apparently be stuck on a plateau. One afternoon while we were walking home along the busy, noisy streets, Eddie became very thoughtful. When we reached a narrow lane and the noise of the traffic had lessened sufficiently, he said, 'You know, I feel like giving up. I'm getting nowhere. I'm at the same point I was a week ago.' I could say nothing to encourage him as I was feeling exactly the same. We moped along. Then, within a matter of five minutes or so, we felt enthusiastic once more. This was completely unexpected. Eddie mirrored my thoughts by saying, 'I'm sure someone at home in South Africa is praying for us!' That afternoon in the language laboratory, earphones clamped to our heads, the fresh impetus carried us through the work that had been set for us. From that time our learning skills certainly improved.

Living in the garage at Study House was not as bad as we had feared it might be. At least we had our own toilet and shower facilities, so we never needed to queue as the single lady missionaries had to do in the main house. We saw them at meals, of course, and got to know them all. Two young women from Canada would not speak to us at all until after they had eaten their breakfast – as we found out when we greeted them pleasantly as they descended the stairs one morning. After they had finished their breakfast they started conversing in a normal sociable manner.

Eddie and I had heard much about the need to pray for missionaries facing 'culture shock' in a strange country, but we agreed that in some ways 'missionary shock' was possibly harder to get over. For instance, just before our supper was brought in from the kitchen one evening, the Study House hostess stood up with a broad smile on her face and made an announcement: 'Well, folk, we're all very privileged tonight. We have to thank Diane and her aunt for our special evening meal!' Diane was one of our language students who had gone out the previous evening with her aunt, who had come to visit her from Canada. Eddie and I were curious, of course, but were surprised when the supper was brought in and we found it consisted of slices of bread covered with small pieces of cooked beef and swimming in gravy. We were even less appreciative when Diane herself told all at the table, 'When my aunt took me out for a meal last night there was a lot of meat and gravy left over, so we asked for a couple of doggy bags to bring back!'

One night we simply could not sleep. A tomcat started yowling in the street from about midnight. The sound came through terribly clearly to us in the wooden garage. We waited for his penetrating calls to stop, but he simply continued until Eddie finally lost patience, filled a bucket with water and went outside in his pyjama shorts, ready to fling his bucketful over the offending cat. Eddie left his bed quietly so as not to disturb the children, who were with us on holiday, and went out of the main gate, his bare feet not making a sound. Just as he rounded the corner of the garage he saw a vague blur of movement and hurled the water in that direction. Simultaneously, some water drenched him with a splash. Out of the darkness came a soft voice, immediately recognisable as Ulrich's. 'Is that you, Eddie? We had the same idea then!' Ulrich had crept out of a side gate with his bucket. Both men were soaked. The offending cat had disappeared, still as dry as a bone.

After only four months of language study we were told we were urgently needed as doctors in a small hospital in Central Thailand, called Nongbua. We would therefore not be able to complete the year of language study that was allowed by OMF to all new missionaries. I objected to this proposal, pointing out that we were not yet fully conversant with the Thai language. I reminded the Bangkok Superintendent, Cyril Falconer, that when Hudson Taylor had founded the China Inland Mission he had made facility with language the very first priority for its missionaries. My objection was summarily overruled. Cyril replied, 'Just do as you're told!'

With small bags containing clothing and other personal items, Eddie and I caught a train to Chumsaeng, from where we could go by bus to Nongbua, about 40 miles further on. The bus was old and shabby, with narrow seats and hardly any legroom. We were fortunate to find two seats next to each other on the right-hand side. Our feet were raised up on two four-gallon tins full of fresh fish packed in ice. The floor beneath these tins was wet through from the melting ice, and the fishy smell made me gag. There was no use protesting – the bus was grossly overcrowded, with all available floor space crammed with goods for trading in the villages. Once we had left the station, most of the other passengers, all Thai, leaned back and went to sleep. (We had not previously noticed this engaging characteristic of the Thai, but they love to take catnaps whenever they can – perhaps because they all rise very early in the morning.) Others started to open packages of food, exchanging choice morsels with other passengers. Those who stayed awake conducted loud and lively conversations, their strident tones easily heard over the noise of the bus's old engine. It was very hot and dry and all the windows were wide open to try to catch any possible breeze.

Some hours went by with frustrating sluggishness, the scenery of flat rice plains unchanging. Eventually we reached a bridge, mostly made of tree trunks. This bridge had partly collapsed in the middle and was now shaped like a great V. We inched onto the bridge as the driver tried to negotiate the acute angle in the middle, but the rear of the bus scraped ominously. We had only travelled a short distance on the other side of the bridge when the bus came to a stop. Why had it stopped? What had happened? We could only wonder, while the imperturbable Thai simply sat and waited. After about an hour a second orange bus came towards us and stopped opposite ours, with only a couple of inches separating the vehicles. The road was completely blocked. The two drivers spoke to each other through their windows and then the conductor and driver of the newly arrived bus got out and went to the rear of their vehicle.

At last a fellow passenger took pity on us and explained that we had a puncture, but no spare wheel.

'But what is the other bus doing here?' asked Eddie.

'Oh, they have a spare wheel,' came the reply.

'But why are our driver and conductor sitting in our bus, while the driver and conductor of the new bus are out replacing our wheel?'

'Because it's *their* spare wheel!' This was said in a way that made us feel stupid. 'They'll pick up our punctured tyre for repair when they've finished changing the wheel, and then leave it for us at the bus station.'

While the two buses remained side by side, the passengers from both buses brought out fruit and other delicacies, sharing them amongst one another. Although Eddie and I had not brought any food for the journey, we were pressed amiably to accept some of their food by cheerful passengers on the bus just two inches away from our window.

The puncture episode made us three and a half hours late for our scheduled arrival, so it was already dark when we reached Nongbua. Fortunately, Dr Ursula Loewenthal, who met us, was used to happenings of this kind and was not in the least upset by our unpunctuality. Ursula was the only doctor at Nongbua Hospital. She was due to be away for about six weeks and had asked for us to replace her while she was gone.

Before Ursula left she familiarised us with aspects of the work in the hospital and introduced us to the Thai staff. She then took us to a small wooden house on stilts that was to be our quarters, and left us alone. We looked through the house curiously. When we reached the bedroom we happened to look up – only to see a moderately large snake lying along a beam on the wall in the bedroom. We recoiled in horror and called Lefty Reid, the hospital handyman, to come and look. He told us it was a very poisonous banded krait and he would have to destroy it. Eddie bravely anchored the snake where it was with a broom and Lefty killed it with practised skill.

That afternoon, while we stood on the small veranda looking out over the rice fields that surrounded the house, we saw an eight-foot-long black cobra. The rice had recently been harvested, leaving short stalks, and the snake was easily visible as it slithered between the stalks. Once more we cried out anxiously for Lefty. He took one look at the snake with its spread hood and ran to fetch a can of paraffin, which he hurled into the grass surrounding the house. He then set fire to it. The resultant conflagration was spectacular, though Eddie and I could not really enjoy the display. We were too worried that the house might be burnt down. When the fire had died down, the snake, of course, had disappeared – more likely to have fled the scene than to have been killed.

The days passed quickly and uneventfully and almost before we realised it, it was time for Dr Ursula to return. We thankfully handed back to her the responsibility for the hospital and made preparations to leave. But we were not to go back to language school in Bangkok, we learned, much to our disappointment. A crisis had developed in Manorom Hospital because of a lack of doctors, and we were to go there and join the team – for how long, we did not know. So we packed up again and got on a bus to Manorom, also in Central Thailand.

8

'Lightning Heart'

Take my life, and let it be
Consecrated, Lord, to Thee.
(Frances Ridley Havergal)

We arrived at Manorom village at midday in sweltering heat to find Dr Arthur Pennington, the Medical Superintendent, waiting for us. An Australian in his mid thirties, handsome, dark-haired and with an engaging grin, he gave us a warm welcome and took us to what was to be our new home. When we got there, we saw a rather dilapidated wooden house on stilts, partly surrounded by a broken fence. In fact, the only part of its fence that had not collapsed was the gate and its gateposts. The ruins of the fence itself were lost in straggling weeds. It was blisteringly hot that day and we gratefully followed Arthur up the rickety steps and into the house.

'The other missionaries in Manorom Hospital have been thinking of you,' Arthur said, 'and they've boiled some water in preparation for your coming, and put it in the fridge. I'll go and get some for you now.'

Our mouths were so dry with thirst that we could barely

reply. We sat on a rattan couch in the main room and waited eagerly for the promised ice-cold water. But very soon Arthur was back, shaking his head in disappointment.

'I'm afraid that the water is still too hot – your fridge is broken!' he announced. 'But I'll go to the hospital quickly and bring you some iced boiled water from outpatients.'

With that he left us, returning after a few minutes with a large bottle, wet with condensation from the icy water inside it. What a glorious drink that water was! After Arthur had left us, we explored our new home. The first thing we discovered was that our only source of water was a tap on the rear wall of the house, accessible from the back veranda. Its water was yellowish and hazy. We soon learned from other missionaries to drop a lump of alum into a full container of water. When the water became a clearer yellow, we decanted it and boiled it, storing it until it was needed, for cooking, drinking or brushing our teeth. For washing we used the water as it was, from a large Ali Baba jar in the bathroom-cum-toilet. Of course, the repair of the fridge was a priority, even though it depleted our already small quarterly allowance from OMF.

Almost all the houses in Central Thailand were built of teak on wooden stilts to allow better circulation of air and to protect them from flooding during the heavy rains in the monsoon months. There were other advantages to these houses, too, I found. One was that sweeping the floor was a lark: I used a one-handed 'broom' made of a piece of wood with a curved end that was set with whiskery fronds, and simply swished it to and fro as I walked up and down each room. I had no need of dustpan and brush. The dust simply fell through the cracks between the floorboards to the earth below. The spaces between floorboards gave another advantage in the bathroom, we discovered. At first we were nonplussed at the absence of a drain and waste pipe, but then realised there was no need for these: water from the 'shower' simply ran down through the cracks to fall to the ground below. This meant that Eddie and I were reasonably sure we would not have unexpected visitors if one of us was having a shower, because from outside the house the falling water showed that it was an inconvenient time to call.

We were a little taken aback to find that, although the house had been furnished for our family, there was only one upright chair. We were even more surprised when Eddie sat on this chair and it promptly collapsed! Over the weeks and months we gradually saved enough money to buy some sturdier, folding chairs from a nearby town, Nakorn Sawan.

In that part of Central Thailand drainage of sewage was a problem. Next to the Thai-style toilet (almost on a level with the floor) was a covered plastic bucket. This receptacle was for used toilet paper, as to flush it down the loo was certain to cause a major blockage. The OMF provided a house-help for each missionary home and Buasri, our house-help, would empty this bucket and dispose of the paper inside it. Unfortunately, the steps at the rear of our home had fallen down, so Buasri[1] had to carry the bucket down the steps at the front of the house, in full view of our neighbours.

We new missionaries had been warned to be gentle with our house-helps, and to be very tactful in correcting them. One day I returned at lunchtime, tired out from my work at

---

[1] Beautiful lotus.

the hospital, and sat on the rattan couch. Buasri had cleaned the room that very morning. As I stood up my eyes fell on the space behind the couch, only to see a generous number of lacy spider's webs connecting the back of the couch with the wooden beams of the wall. *What can I do?* I thought anxiously. *I don't want to live in a dirty house, but I don't want to upset Buasri.* Then, in a flash of inspiration, I had the answer. 'Buasri,' I called, 'what kind of spiders do you have in Thailand? You cleaned this room this morning, but just look at how the spiders have spun webs again since then!' Buasri never neglected her dusting again after that.

Although Buasri was not all that efficient, she was always willing and pleasant. She got to know me, and what Eddie called my 'Mediterranean' temperament, very well. One day she told me she had a good nickname for me: *jye fai faa* ('lightning heart'). Much as I would have liked to be called by a slightly more flattering name, I could not help but agree with her assessment of my character. That description has remained with me for years, however hard I try to remain placid. One good thing, however, is that although I can get agitated quickly, my annoyance subsides just as rapidly. That, I know, is a source of comfort to my long-suffering husband and children.

When the children arrived on holiday from Chefoo School, the monsoon season had already started. Mornings were often dry, but in the afternoons without fail the rain pelted down in huge, heavy drops. We found that our old house leaked badly; in fact the only room that was fairly leak-proof was our bedroom. When it rained at night the drops made such a clatter on the roof that the din always woke me, however tired I was. I would get out of bed and hurry to the children's room. There I would find two children huddled together in the lower bed of the double bunk unit in an effort to avoid the drops falling from the ceiling, while the third child would be trying to squeeze in with them too. Rainwater already lay in pools in the other rooms. I would bundle the children off to our room and put mats down for them on the parts of the floor that were dry. We got used to this routine without grumbling. Our reward was the drop in temperature that always followed the heavy rain.

On the children's second holiday with us, they were excited and pleased to find that Eddie had bought a plastic swimming pool, which he set up on our back veranda. From a nearby gutter, via an extension he'd had made, the water from the monsoon rains would pour into the pool, filling it to overflowing within a matter of minutes. From that time on, whenever we were woken by rain at night, whatever the time, the whole family changed into bathing suits and wallowed happily in the cool water. No splashing was too much. Whatever water spilled out of the pool, it was instantly replaced from the gushing gutter.

Eddie will never forget the nerve-racking experience of facing his very first patient in the outpatient clinic of Manorom Hospital. Before he went to his allotted examination room, the sister in charge came to him and said sympathetically, 'Dr Rose, I am giving you a nurse interpreter, as you do not yet know enough Thai.' Eddie was glad to have the small, shy nurse aide with him.

The first patient that day was a little old lady who was busily chewing *betel* nut.[2] She sat in the patient's chair and

---

[2] A small black nut with narcotic properties.

immediately began talking volubly in spite of the *betel* nut in her mouth. Not understanding one word, Eddie looked blankly at the nurse aide, who responded with a single word, 'Leg.'

Eddie looked at the patient again, this time noticing that she had a grubby rag tied around her ankle. 'I'd like to examine your leg,' he said in his best Thai, knowing that in this country it was not polite to touch a patient unless one first asked permission to do so. The old lady took no notice. She simply opened her mouth and expectorated a long red stream of *betel* nut juice accurately into the spittoon in the centre of the room, placed there for such an occasion. For a moment, Eddie was lost in admiration at her effortless feat.

Then he spoke again. 'I'd like to examine your leg.' Still she made no response.

He turned again to the nurse aide for help, who said another single word, 'Deaf.' *Oh*, he thought, *so that's the explanation! I'll have to raise my voice. . .*

With that, he thundered, 'I'D LIKE TO EXAMINE YOUR LEG!'

As soon as he had spoken, the little lady shot up out of her chair and shuffled out of the room as fast as she could. Eddie glanced at the nurse aide in bewilderment, only to find her trying hard not to giggle, covering her mouth with her hand. Soon she gave up the struggle, and in spite of it being extremely rude for a nurse to laugh at a doctor, she slipped outside the room, where she could give vent to her feelings.

Now Eddie was completely alone in the room. He did not know what he should do. Finally he also left the room and went in search of the sister. When he found her, she already knew what had happened. 'Dr Rose,' she said, 'the first two times you spoke to the patient to ask her if you could examine her leg, you spoke perfect Thai. But the next time you spoke, you raised your voice and changed the tones of the words – and said you wanted to kill her!'

A couple of days later Eddie asked the nursing staff whether they had seen the old lady again, but she never returned to the hospital. His very first patient at Manorom was lost to him for ever!

Eddie's first sermon was also a bit of a disaster, due to our inadequate language preparation and ability. His chosen subject was 'Good News' and he preached as eloquently as he could about the great good news of the gospel and salvation through faith in Christ. The audience sat quietly, too polite to ask him what he was talking about. It happened that, because of a mistake in the tone of a word, he had been preaching about 'Good Rice'. The nonplussed hearers could not understand why he wanted to tell them about good rice. After all, everyone knew that Thailand had the best rice in the world!

After two months had passed, we found that our monthly electricity bill had shot up and was disconcertingly high. Eddie mentioned this to some missionary colleagues and they advised him to check the main supply line, just outside our home. When he went to look, he was stunned to find a neat device taped to our electricity supply line, bleeding off our electricity to the neighbour's house. No wonder the amount on our bill had rocketed.

In our home in Manorom, simple as it was, Eddie felt acutely the lack of a piano. All his life up to now had been dominated by music. He was musical with every fibre of his being, singing, playing the piano and organ. Here, the humidity and heat militated against our having a piano, and in any case we could not dream of buying one. So, although he said nothing to me of this hunger for music, Eddie was inwardly pining. He was all the more pleased, therefore, when the chaplain of the nearby US Air Force base at the town of Taakli asked him to go over every night for a week to play the organ for a series of evangelistic meetings. To Eddie, playing each evening in the chapel was as refreshing as a glass of iced water to a man lost in a desert.

Some months later, a jeep pulled up in front of the hospital. A soldier emerged, holding a bulky object wrapped in sacking. 'For Dr Rose,' he said. The parcel was duly handed over to Eddie, who opened it with curiosity. As he pulled away the last of the wrappings his face showed his astonishment and delight: there was a guitar, complete with a leather patch on it, with the letters 'OMF' burnt into it. Eddie had never played a guitar before. Carefully he put it away on the top shelf of a cupboard in the living room, to be used on some future occasion.

One day Eddie could not bear his longing to make music any longer. He stopped his preparation for a talk in Thai he was to give at morning prayers at the hospital, stood up and took out the guitar. With his natural flair for music, he was soon idly strumming on the guitar while he sang softly to himself. Meanwhile, I was at the desk in the next room, typing away. When his music penetrated my consciousness I left the typewriter and went to the door. The tune he was playing was unfamiliar to me – it was obviously one of his improvisations – but I recognised the words. Eddie sang softly but with a poignancy that made my heart ache. The fatigue at the end of a busy day; the frustrations we had met in our work at the hospital; the feeling of helplessness against the weight of ignorance and superstition – all these emotions were washed out of me as I listened. In their place came peace. The words Eddie was singing were those of the well-known and much-loved hymn, 'Take My Life'. I found myself singing softly along with him in muted harmony:

> Take my life, and let it be
> Consecrated, Lord, to Thee.
> Take my moments and my days. . .
>
> Take my hands. . .
> Take my feet. . .

Our spirits were lifted and renewed as we returned to the hospital next morning. Even though our language was still woefully inadequate, we managed to cope.

One morning the hospital Superintendent, Dr Arthur Pennington, called us to his office and told us that we were going to be allowed to go back to Bangkok to finish our interrupted language study. How we rejoiced! We had feared that we would never be able to go back because of the continued shortage of doctors at the hospital, and that our language skills would therefore never be sufficient. With light hearts we returned home that evening to pack our belongings, looking forward to acquiring really good Thai so that we would be better able to communicate with patients, both medically and spiritually.

9

Language, Fire and Flood

They will speak with new tongues.
(Mark 16:17)

The head teacher of the Union Language School in Bangkok arranged to see us in her office. We enjoyed being able to exchange chit-chat with her. Later we found out that this interview had been an oral examination in spoken Thai. If we had known that at the start of the interview we would have been tongue-tied with fright.

As a result of that interview we were considered able to take the first year's final examinations with our original class, even though these exams were to take place within three weeks of our return to the language school. In order to catch up with the other students, we now had to work very, very hard for the next three weeks. Our study times were doubled and each day we endured six hours of tuition and six hours of home study. The weeks flew by until it was time to do the written and oral examinations. The Lord was good to us and we both passed – Eddie came first and I came second. Then, when the rest of our class packed up and went to their designated places of work, Eddie and I stayed on for three more months: we had not yet had the twelve months' tuition that OMF arranged for every new missionary.

During this time of language study in Bangkok we lived in a small wooden house, one of a row in the same lane as the larger Study House where new missionaries lived during their first year in Thailand. With us were two senior lady missionaries, Minka Hanskamp and Margaret Morgan, who had come to refresh their Thai language abilities after years in South Thailand. We were glad to get to know them and enjoyed their friendship. Little did we know then that, years later, they would be abducted by Communist bandits in the jungle of South Thailand and made to kneel down before their captors, to be shot in the head. Their witness to the Lord and their faithfulness even to death made a huge impact on many hearts.

There were six people in our new class: two American businessmen, two American lady missionaries, Eddie and myself. The two businessmen were from Texas and simply could not understand a word of the Thai language, even after a year of basic teaching. When the teacher gestured to them, they would turn their heads to look at each other and then say, 'What d'you think she means, Hank?' in a broad Southern drawl. Eventually they both gave up trying to learn Thai and left the class. Eddie met Hank in the street in Bangkok some years later and found him happily teaching English to Thai colleagues. After the two businessmen left the class, Eddie was once again the only man in it. We women, though sorry for him in a way, were glad he was always the first to be asked. It meant we had more time to think before our turn came to answer.

In this more advanced class we learned to use Thai

idioms and the particular 'high' language used to speak of the king or of God. We were also considered able to read books more advanced than the basic primers we had used in the first year, so now we also read from a Thai novel. The day we started on this novel, Eddie was asked first as usual to begin reading aloud. He managed well and this helped the rest of us. At the end of that lesson we were told to study the chapter again and to prepare sentences of our own, using some of the words we had read that were new to us. The next morning in class our teacher looked up at Eddie and said, 'Môr[1] Rose, will you give us an example of the sentences you prepared yesterday?' Eddie became ashen, his heart in his boots – he had completely forgotten that homework assignment! He looked about desperately, his eye falling on his three fellow students. Suddenly he remembered one of the new words we had read the previous day, *mianoi*[2], and he relaxed. In Thai he introduced the teacher to his wife (me) and to his two mistresses (the two missionary ladies). Too late he realised what a shocking effect his light-hearted jest had had on the two earnest single ladies who shared our class. Apologies, however sincere, were not enough. Within a matter of days these two women asked for a transfer to another class, where they were unlikely to be subjected to such 'abuse'.

Another (unintentional) escapade made Eddie famous throughout the school. At that time several classes were held in various parts of a very large room. Distances between classes ensured a reasonable amount of privacy for each group. We were reading from a Thai book called *Ryang*

---

[1] 'Doctor'.

[2] 'Secondary wife'; 'mistress'.

Phrajesu.[3] Because this book was written about Jesus Christ, the Son of God, it was written in the 'high' Thai language. Once again the teacher chose Eddie to read first. He managed the reading well in spite of the many unfamiliar words it contained, because he knew the basic rules of pronunciation. But then – as Eddie's face rapidly paled – the teacher instructed him to lay his book face down on the table and say out loud what he had just read, using any of the 'high' words he could remember.

Eddie looked up at the ceiling, then all about him before sitting up straight and replying, *'Tootsawan haj Maria naarok!'* There was an electric hush in every class in the large room. All the teachers looked at one another in horror and then stared incredulously at Eddie. Our own teacher could not utter a sound. We looked across the table at each other, wondering what on earth was wrong. Some of the teachers started to titter in embarrassment. Finally we persuaded our teacher, *Khruu* Pridaa, to tell us what dreadful thing Eddie had said. In a very subdued voice she murmured, '*Môr* Rose said that the angel gave Mary *hell.*' What a thing for a missionary to say! How did Eddie manage to come up with such a terrible statement? Eddie had wanted to say, 'The angel gave Mary a baby.' His first words were correct, but unfortunately for him, the high word for 'baby' was *taarok* and the letter 't' at the beginning was shaped just like a lower-case 'n' in English. So he pronounced the word as *naarok*, and that meant 'hell'.

One night we were woken in the small hours by Minka Hanskamp shouting agitatedly, 'Fire! Fire! You must get up

---

[3] 'Stories of Jesus'.

and out of the house! Quickly! Get up! Get dressed and take your passports and run!' Bewildered and scared, we dressed hastily, grabbed our passports and left the house. As we huddled together in the street Minka told us of memories that had flooded back of the war in Holland when she was a young girl, and how initially she had been convinced by the cracking noises and red glow outside that war had come to Thailand. The dark night was all but banished by an ominous flickering glow. We could hear panic-stricken voices all about us. A house three doors away from ours was well and truly on fire. Because all the homes in this lane were made of wood, our own house was threatened too.

We had never been in a situation like this before and our hearts were hammering with excitement and anxiety. We ventured into the dark lane to find out what we could. The narrow lane was filled with people, some dressed and some still in their nightclothes. More people kept crowding into the street as they fled their threatened homes. At last a fire engine arrived – but no one knew of a supply of water that it could use. (The fire engines in Thailand at that time were equipped with hoses and pumps, but were not supplied with water reservoirs.) Seeing Eddie, the firemen asked him if he knew where they could pump up water to douse the fire. Fortunately, Eddie remembered that there was a canal in the grounds of Study House, almost opposite the fiercely burning house. He opened the gates and gestured the driver to enter. Soon the firemen's large-bore hose was slurping up the water, lowering the level of the canal steadily as they fought the blaze. By this time two houses had been gutted.

As Eddie returned to where I was standing, a little old Thai lady caught his eye. She was standing next to the hose as it crossed from one side of the lane to the other, with a bucket at her feet. As he looked more closely to see what she was doing, he could not help smiling to himself. The frugal old woman was collecting drops of water as they leaked steadily from a defect in the hose. Her full attention was on what she was doing, and she was not interested at all in the raging flames not far away. Fortunately the fire was contained before it spread any further to all the wooden houses in the lane, so our home was left unharmed.

A week or two after the fire Eddie was walking down the lane where the metal lampposts along the side were still tilted and bent from the fierce heat of the fire. He glanced at the blackened, desolate area, wondering when new homes would be constructed to house the families left without shelter. To his amazement, standing out in pristine splendour in a corner of each plot of ground were brightly painted spirit houses, roofs painted with gold leaf gleaming in the sunlight. The incongruity of these fresh, bright structures in the midst of blackened ash and destruction struck him forcibly.

All Buddhist homes in Thailand, and many businesses and stores too, have the obligatory spirit houses, usually in a corner of the garden. Sometimes, in the case of a commercial building such as a bank or a department store, the spirit house will be placed on top of the roof. These spirit houses are small, temple-shaped miniature buildings on a pedestal and are there to propitiate the evil spirits that the Thai fear abysmally. Inside the structure are offerings of rice or other food, and the sacred lotus or another flower is often draped over them.

Wondering at the priorities of the Thai, Eddie stopped and asked the first person he saw why these structures had been built first, while whole families were still homeless. 'But of course the spirit houses had to be built first!' was the reply. 'The spirits can't have been satisfied with the ones that were there and so they started the fire. We dare not build new wooden houses until the spirits are satisfied.'

When we were near the end of our additional language study, the monsoon rains arrived. They brought downpours heavier than we had ever experienced before, which started and stopped with disconcerting suddenness. In the afternoons the heavy bouts of rain left some lanes and streets under 8 inches of opaque, dirty water. At home in South Africa, puddles of rainwater were always clear. This contrast made me realise, as nothing else could, what a filthy place Bangkok actually was.

It was not very long before the lane in front of our home was flooded too. This lasted for weeks. The garden was under 18 inches of dirty, yellowish water, so we had to place large stones along the path from the gate to the house and use them gingerly as stepping stones. For the first time we could understand fully why so many houses in Thailand are built on stilts. Fortunately, the main part of the house was safely above the level of the floods. I remember standing on the front veranda one afternoon after school, idly watching the water lapping at the steps, when to my astonishment I saw several goldfish swimming happily past the house. The obvious explanation eluded me until I heard that a neighbour's fishpond had been flooded and all his goldfish had been swept away. On another occasion I saw the sinuous black form of a snake in the water below the steps to our front door.

There was a banana tree in our garden. During the floods I noticed that it was bearing a bunch of ripe bananas. I was alone in the house and wondered how I could pick the delicious fruit. I took a light folding table and a metal chair and then braved the unknown dangers of the murky waters, my heart in my mouth. It was not the depth of the water that worried me, but the fact that it was not clear enough for me to see if there were any snakes in my path. The trip to the bananas was not long, but it seemed to me to take for ever. I gingerly put down the table and then placed the chair next to it. By climbing on the chair and then onto the table I was just able to reach the bananas that hung so tantalisingly high up in the tree. Triumphantly I grasped the bananas with one hand as I carried the folded table and chair under my arms, and made my way cautiously back to the half-submerged steps of the house. If I had taken time to think clearly, I do not think I would have made that risky essay into the flooded garden for such a small reward as a bunch of bananas, especially in a land where bananas grew wild and were dirt cheap and easy to buy!

At last our months of language study came to an end. We welcomed the thought of leaving crowded, noisy Bangkok for the peace of the countryside. We found we were looking forward to being back at the Manorom Hospital compound again, surrounded by green rice fields. This time we knew beforehand where we would be working and this made the move much more pleasant. We were not disturbed by the thought of the uncomfortable, rickety old bus in which we were to travel; we were even looking forward to seeing the road surface once again through the holes in the floor of the bus. It was still a novel experience for us. Happily we packed and got ready for Manorom, where we were to work for the next three years.

10

'You've Lost Your Witness!'

Then you shall return.
(Joshua 1:15)

When we arrived back in Manorom we were glad to find that we had been allotted a different house. It was more comfortable, in a much better state of repair and even had a garden. It had become available for us because the missionaries who had previously occupied it had returned home to Denmark. We were overjoyed to be able to live there. The kitchen, dining area and bathroom were in a separate building from the lounge and bedrooms. There were even ceiling fans in some of the rooms and this greatly increased our comfort. The roof was in a much better condition and we found that even the heaviest monsoon rains did not penetrate it. It was so much better not having to get up in the middle of the night to find dry spots for the children when they were with us on holiday that we did not even miss our midnight swims.

Our landlady was notorious in Manorom for having once knifed a would-be robber to death. Although she had been

sentenced to years of imprisonment for her crime, she had
not served one day in jail. She had convinced the police that
she was far too important a member of the local society to
be imprisoned. Instead, she suggested that her mother go to
jail on her behalf and serve the sentence by proxy. The
police accepted this offer, and her mother was put in jail. No
wonder people went about in fear of this redoubtable lady!

A short time before we arrived, the landlady's cat had
produced a litter. One of these kittens was much smaller
than the others, and had suffered some kind of injury to its
spine. Its hind legs could not function so it dragged itself
along, using just its two front paws. Naturally it always lost
out when the other, stronger kittens wanted to feed; it was
always just too slow. I felt sorry for this little mite, and one
day I spoke to the landlady, offering to put the kitten to
sleep with an anaesthetic. Immediately she bristled and
responded with an emphatic 'No!'.

When I told Eddie how she had reacted he was not surprised. 'You've forgotten that Buddhism doesn't permit the
killing of any animal,' he reminded me. 'They believe firmly
in reincarnation, and anyone who does not live a good life
may be reincarnated as an animal as punishment. So if you
killed the kitten you might be murdering someone who
lived long ago and now has been reborn as the kitten. Of
course, the person must have lived a bad life, to be reborn
with such a physical deformity.'

I digested this in silence, feeling embarrassed at my lack
of sensitivity towards our landlady. Nevertheless, one day
not long after I had offered to ease the kitten from its suffering, she came to me, making sure no one else was within
earshot. 'Will you please do as you suggested, and put that

kitten to sleep?' she asked. 'I can't go on looking at it suffering – it's going to die of starvation, anyway.' And I did so, in great secrecy, in case others should find out.

To illustrate the lengths to which the Thai would go to avoid actually killing an animal, let me tell you what once happened. A Thai family who lived near the sea had a dog they did not want to keep any more – perhaps it was vicious, or perhaps it just barked too much at night. What could they do? They could not simply put it down. That was unthinkable. So the famous Thai ingenuity came into play. They took the dog with them to the seashore one day at low tide and tied it to a stake they had stuck firmly in the sand near the water's edge. Then they trooped back to their house. Of course, when the tide came in, the dog drowned. Nonetheless, their principles remained intact. They had not killed the dog – the sea had.

The same attitude even applied to the killing of poisonous snakes. Some years later Eddie had gone to the local post office, but had found it deserted. He waited for a few minutes and then, hearing some voices outside the side door, went to investigate. He found the post office staff and customers intently watching a small cobra. One of the clerks had a piece of fine string, at the end of which he had tied a loop. He was endeavouring to put the loop around the snake just behind its head. While this was going on, all thought of work left their heads. At last the clerk's patience was rewarded and the loop slipped neatly over the little snake's head. Triumphantly he lifted up the string, from which the snake dangled helplessly, and tied the other end to one of the washing lines that were strung at the side of the post office property. Satisfied, they all trooped back into the post office and the afternoon's work was resumed. Eddie was a bit perplexed, but finally he realised the meaning of the drama he had just witnessed. By simply hanging up the snake, it would surely starve to death – but the clerk was innocent of its killing.

Once, Eddie had gone by train to see a professor of surgery at a Bangkok hospital. The professor was not yet there, so his secretary showed Eddie into the office to wait. Eddie's eye was drawn to a photograph on the wall, a close-up of a bright green snake with a bright red-tipped tail. He recognised the snake as one of the most poisonous indigenous snakes in Thailand, and he moved closer to the picture, wondering how it had been possible for the photographer to get so close to the snake. 'I see you've noticed my photograph,' said the professor, entering the office. 'I took that photo myself in my garden. Lovely, isn't it? We Thai are so very different from you foreigners! If you had seen that snake in your garden you would have killed it straight away. We Thai would never do that. We would let it live. It might be the reincarnation of someone who has died.'

The Thai are very fond of fish, poultry and pork. Killing chickens and pigs for eating is exempt of all blame. They eat much less beef – perhaps because the older generations of Thai, especially those of Chinese extraction, will not eat beef under any circumstance. They will tell you that chickens, fish or pigs do not 'work' for humans, while water buffalo do. They say it is not fair to reward a faithful servant (the water buffalo) by killing and eating him in the end.

We found that driving a car in Manorom was very different from driving at home in South Africa. Here, should an accident occur, the size of the vehicles concerned was more important than who was actually to blame. Once I was riding our 50cc motorcycle up the lane leading to Manorom Hospital, with a huge lorry laden with Coca-Cola bottles in front of me. The driver was delivering bottles to various tiny shops on each side of the lane. Suddenly, without warning, he stopped his lorry in my path. I could not stop in time and my motorbike went right into his rear. The damage to each vehicle was minor, but nevertheless the accident was reported to the police. A week later I received a call to attend the police station. When I arrived there, I found the lorry driver waiting. I had expected to be asked whether or not I had been riding too close to the lorry, but no time was wasted in apportioning blame. Right there in front of me the lorry driver was summarily fined, simply because his was the larger vehicle.

Some years earlier, the hospital driver had had an accident involving the ambulance van and another vehicle. He reported the incident to the hospital Superintendent, Dr Pennington, and honestly owned up to the fact that he had been to blame. Dr Pennington spoke to the chief of police and told him that the hospital driver had been at fault and that the hospital would pay for any damage or fine. 'No, that won't be right,' the police chief reassured him. 'You are a Christian hospital – you cannot be to blame! It's all right. Both vehicles are insured and the insurance will pay.' Arthur Pennington insisted, however, that it was only right that the hospital should pay as their driver had been in the wrong. 'If you insist,' said the nonplussed police chief, 'the matter will have to be referred to court.' Dr Pennington then asked when that hearing would be, and was given a date and time that he wrote down in his diary. On the appointed day and at the appointed time Arthur appeared at the court. He waited and waited, but the expected court case did not begin. Eventually he spoke to one of the court officials. 'When is the case involving our hospital's driver beginning?' he asked. 'O-o-oh!' smiled the official. 'I wondered what you were doing here! That case was heard yesterday. When you did not turn up we realised that you were too busy with important affairs at the hospital, so we proceeded without you. The case was settled amicably and the insurance agreed to pay.'

The children came to stay with us for their seven-week-long school holidays twice a year. At the end of each school term they were desperately impatient to go home, while at the end of each holiday they were glad to be going back to school. I felt that they had probably had enough of parental discipline after so many weeks at home, while Eddie and I were rather looking forward to the peace and quiet that would follow their return to school. While they were in the wooden house it reverberated and quivered with life. It seemed as if it was never still.

One afternoon, during the hottest time of the year, while the thermometer in the living room registered 104°F, I was sitting on the floor cutting out a dress. I'd had to turn off the ceiling fan to stop the pattern pieces from blowing away. Perspiration dripped from my face and arms and made it almost impossible to keep from staining the pieces of cotton material. Suddenly Anthony erupted into the room, his voice breaking into my concentration.

'Mom, have you got any small things around that you don't need?' When I did not reply at once, he asked insistently, 'Have you, Mom?'

I looked up from my work. 'What kind of small things are you thinking of?' I asked. 'What do you need them for?'

'Oh, Jen and Sue and me – here they come now!' And Anthony dodged out of the girls' way as they hurtled breathlessly into the room, scattering my pattern and material. 'Jen and Sue and me have sold all our old toys and people still want to buy more things. We thought that perhaps you would have something we could sell.'

'Sold your toys? Where on earth have you been selling them?'

'Oh, down at the market!' The expression on his face was eloquent. *Where else could we have sold them?* 'We borrowed a bike and took things and made a kind of stall. People passing us stopped to look, and bought everything. Lots more people came and now we need more stuff to sell!'

'But you can't speak Thai! How do you tell the people the prices of the things you're selling?'

'I *know* we can't speak Thai, but we do know *nyng, song, saam,*[1] and if it's more than three baht we show them with our fingers, like this.' Anthony spread his fingers to show me.

'And an old lady bought my old doll Mary for eight baht!' burst out an excited Jennifer.

'Quiet, Jennifer!' Anthony said. 'Mom's going to find something more for us to sell.'

In the face of his supreme confidence in me I could not refuse him. I agreed to look through our meagre possessions, though I was doubtful of success. After searching as thoroughly as I could, I had collected only a small pile of

---

[1] 'One, two, three'.

articles. All I had managed to find were three handker-
chiefs, a small notebook, two coloured pencils (made in
Japan) and a rather dilapidated plastic ball. *Surely I can find
something more!* I thought. Eventually I came across a small
parcel, still gift-wrapped, that had been Eddie's present to
me before we left South Africa. I knew what was inside, and
I prized the contents – guest-sized tablets of soap by Lanvin,
scented with my favourite fragrance, Arpege. I could even
smell it through the wrapping paper. This was certainly not
'something I didn't want', but I had to acknowledge to
myself that in our circumstances here in Thailand I could
not say truthfully that I *needed* it. I was in two minds, torn
between giving up my soaps and keeping them. Even as I
argued with myself, I knew in my heart that I had no real
choice. I faced up to the fact that in leaving South Africa for
Thailand as a missionary I had left behind me comfort,
financial security and luxuries like French soap, Italian
shoes and expensive clothes. Finally I had to admit to
myself that this little box and its contents did not belong to
the life we now lived. Watched intently by three pairs of
sparkling eyes, I added the box of soaps to the tiny pile.

'*Thanks*, Mom,' breathed Susan fervently, while the ever-
practical Jennifer said, 'The ladies will *love* this soap – it
smells so good!' Quickly the children put the articles into a
bright red plastic bucket and set off for the market again,
chattering animatedly to each other. I watched them from
my bedroom window as they disappeared down the dusty
road, carrying with them the last token of my old life in
South Africa, and I felt strangely at peace.

Eddie and I both saw people in the outpatients' department in the mornings. After our ward rounds, I was usually

free to go home mid-afternoon, but Eddie generally stayed, because he had extra duties as a specialist general surgeon. His skills were welcomed and as well as doing his stint in the outpatients' department he was often to be found in the operating theatre. There, although he was covered almost completely by his surgical gown, boots, cap and mask, it was still very easy to recognise him. At 6 feet 2 inches, he towered above the tiny Thai nurses and nurse aides. He had to stoop to operate, because even when the operating table had been pumped up as high as it could go it was still too low for him. Nurse assistants at the operations found they could not see over the patient's inert body unless they stood on stools. Even then, they were shorter than Eddie by about 18 inches.

One day, while Eddie was performing a hysterectomy, a sudden gush of arterial blood about 9 inches high erupted in front of his face. An inexperienced nurse aide had inadvertently removed the artery clamp that secured the uterine artery. Shocked into immediate action, Eddie slammed a swab over the haemorrhage and pressed hard. There was no possibility of clamping the artery again, because the cut end of the artery had retracted into the pelvic tissues and was no longer visible. While Eddie applied enough pressure to control the bleeding, he glared at the offending nurse aide and sharply demanded to know why she had removed that clamp – an understandable reaction in the West, but an unforgivable one in Thailand. To humiliate another person in front of her peers is one of the worst things one can do. Later the Thai theatre sister spoke privately to Eddie and explained that he should really not have glared like that (the nurse aide had not intended to do wrong) and, in any case, he should have spoken to her in private when he had cooled down, not in front of the other staff.

Some months later the truth of what the theatre sister had said was brought home forcibly to Eddie when Michael Griffiths, the General Director of OMF, visited Manorom for the annual Field Conference of Central Thailand. Michael asked to see Eddie in private. 'You've lost your witness!' were his opening words. Eddie's eyes opened in shock. The General Director went on, 'The nurses in theatre don't believe in your Christianity – they say you can preach all right, but your actions don't correspond with your words.'

Eddie was stunned. 'But how. . .?' he began to say, when the General Director continued. 'When a nurse does something wrong during an operation, you get cross. You made a nurse lose face in front of everybody in the operating theatre when you bawled her out. Your religion has lost all credibility with the staff. You've lost your witness!'

Speechless, Eddie stared at the General Director's back as he turned and left the room.

Later, feeling shattered and dejected, Eddie dragged his way home and told me what had happened. 'I'm hopeless,' he said. 'We might as well go home. If I've lost my witness, there's no point in staying on here.'

'How did he mean, "lost your witness"?' I demanded. 'I'm often in theatre to give anaesthetics and I haven't noticed anything to make the nurses feel that way.'

'Do you remember the time when I was operating on a difficult case for hysterectomy, and the scrub nurse took off the wrong clamp – the one for the uterine artery? When the blood shot up from the artery and we almost lost the patient from haemorrhage before we could get the bleeding under control?'

'Yes, I certainly remember that case, but the patient came through OK in the end.'

'*She* did, but apparently *I* didn't. I looked daggers at the nurse over my mask and yelled at her for doing such a stupid thing. That's acceptable in South Africa, but not here in Thailand. And the trouble is, I don't think I can behave in any other way. My whole training would be against it. Anyway, it would be against my nature!'

'But Eddie, God can change even your nature, if you only give it to Him,' I pleaded.

'I gave God everything I possessed when we came out to Thailand, but this is my *nature*!' came his desperate reply. 'I was trained to save patients' lives – not to let them die!'

Depressed and fatigued, Eddie was not in any mood for visitors that day, but in the late afternoon Isaac and Eileen Scott came back to our home. They had been staying with us during the Field Conference, which Isaac attended in his capacity as Central Thailand Field Director. After supper I sat with Eileen in the lounge while Eddie and Isaac went to another room where they could talk in private. Eddie told Isaac what Michael Griffiths had said to him and poured out his feelings of utter despair about ever becoming an effective missionary in Thailand, where 'losing face' was apparently more important than losing a life. In due time we all prayed together, and this time of prayer and fellowship brought quiet and peace to our spirits.

After our two guests left, Eddie did not reiterate his statement that it would be better for us to throw in the towel and go back to South Africa. Instead, he was very quiet and thoughtful. Before we got ready for bed we knelt together in prayer. When it was Eddie's turn to pray he opened his heart to the Lord: *Dear Lord, You know how I've lost my witness with the theatre staff; You also know how much I love You. I could promise now never to get cross in theatre again and I'd be able to keep that promise for a few days, but then I know I'd break it again under similar circumstances. And yet I do want to serve You in this place where You have called us. This whole thing is impossible for me in my own strength. I can't change.*

And God's answer came to him: *You never will! But My grace is sufficient. My strength will conquer your permanent weakness.*

And, his head still bowed, Eddie prayed silently, *So, Lord, will You take me now, just as I am, take my nature, take my training, take my self and use me in Your work?*

The Lord heard Eddie's agonised prayer and answered it in a marvellous way, so that the change in his nature became apparent to those who worked with him in the hospital. He became a different man, a more patient and understanding surgeon. Even more marvellous, perhaps, was the fact that no patient on the operating table suffered because of this new attitude. Years later, at a farewell party for theatre staff, everyone concerned was sitting cross-legged on the floor of the corridor leading to the operating theatre. A nurse aide who was sitting next to Eddie turned to him with a puzzled look. 'Doctor,' she said, 'you are not the same man as you were when you first came to Manorom.'

'Oh, yes I am,' Eddie replied. 'But it is Christ in me that you see. Underneath I'm the same person as I was originally – but I have given my old self to the Lord, and He keeps me!'

11

Medicine in Manorom

And a time to heal.
(Ecclesiastes 3:3)

We had been working in Manorom Christian Hospital for about six months when a boy of 16 was admitted with suspected poliomyelitis. Tests showed, however, that he was suffering from a disease called Landry's paralysis, or Guillain Barré syndrome. This meant that his paralysis was not permanent. The treatment for this condition was to give him nursing care and to put him on a respirator when his chest muscles also became affected by the ascending paralysis. After about three weeks, the paralysis would gradually recede and the boy would be completely normal once more. Eddie explained this to the parents, who, although they remained unconvinced, allowed their son to be admitted for treatment. When the boy could not breathe spontaneously any more, he was put on the respirator. The parents were devastated by this development.

'We want to take our son home,' said the father flatly, not

listening to Eddie's protests that the boy was not dying, and would recover fully given time.

Eddie said, 'But you cannot take the hospital's respirator home with you, and without it your son will surely die!'

'But he will die anyway!'

'No, I promise you he will get well.'

'We have to take him now while he is still alive; if he dies the taxi driver will be too frightened of the evil spirits that come from a dead body, and will not allow him into the taxi.'

'But don't you realise,' pleaded Eddie, 'that if we disconnect the respirator now, he will be dead in a few minutes?'

'No! We must take him *now*!'

The parents were adamant, and nothing Eddie could say made any difference. They asked that the boy be taken out to the waiting taxi with the respirator still attached, so that the driver of the taxi could see his chest rising and falling and know he was alive.

'But then we will have to disconnect the respirator and your son really *will* be dead!' Eddie protested.

'By then it won't matter,' came the callous reply. 'By then he will already be inside, and the driver won't know he's carrying a dead body in his taxi!'

And so, with a very heavy heart, Eddie watched the taxi leave the hospital grounds with a dying 16-year-old boy lying on the back seat. It was at times like this that Eddie wondered if his coming to Thailand was worthwhile at all – and whether the rural Thai would ever be liberated from their ignorance and superstitious beliefs.

One day Eddie examined a toddler of two, to find that he was suffering from early pneumonia. Eddie wrote out a prescription for antibiotic syrup for the hospital pharmacy and gave the mother precise instructions on how to administer the medicine. He did not expect to see the mother and child at the hospital again. But three days later he looked up from his desk in outpatients to see the mother coming through the door, cradling her child in her arms, obviously now very ill indeed.

'He's much worse!' she burst out even before she sat in front of the desk, her eyes reproachful.

'Did you give him the medicine syrup exactly as I explained to you?' Eddie asked as he took up his stethoscope ready to examine the child's lungs.

'No. He didn't want to take it,' was her incredible reply.

Once the child had been admitted to hospital and was receiving antibiotics by injection, Eddie had time to discuss the case with a colleague who had worked in Thailand for many years.

'The Thai often do that,' said his friend. 'It's because they believe in reincarnation. If a baby or child refuses to take its medicine, the parents won't insist on giving it. They believe that each baby is born with the spirit of a person who has died and is now reincarnated. If the baby refuses to take medicine, the mother defers to the greater wisdom of the person who now inhabits her child's body and who obviously has more experience of life than she does.'

Another difficulty we met in Manorom Hospital was that patients would first treat themselves, and would come to hospital only as a last resort. Almost all drugs were freely obtainable without prescription. The drugs that patients turned to first we called 'the three Cs' – cortisone, chloromycetin and coramine (a cardiac stimulant). This habit of self-medication often obscured the actual disease from which the patient was suffering and made diagnosis more difficult, but occasionally it had even more serious consequences. This was the case when Eddie was called to see a young man who was complaining of severe pain in his right arm and hand. When Eddie first saw him, he was moaning softly and turning his head from side to side while he cradled his right arm in his left. The supported arm was discoloured and almost black, from the hand to mid-forearm. Sweat beaded his face, which was drawn with pain. Had a snake bitten him? Was it a scorpion sting? All Eddie's questions were met with vague, incoherent mumbling replies, as pain made it impossible for the man to concentrate.

Finally Eddie sent the nurse to find the friend who had brought the man to hospital. The friend soon told Eddie the whole story. It had been neither a snake nor a scorpion that had caused this condition. It had come about simply through the patient's determination to cure himself. He had been feeling off-colour, and went to the local teashop in the market to buy some medicine. A vial of terramycin caught his eye and he bought it, as well as a syringe and a needle. He had heard of terramycin before when a friend of his had been given injections in hospital a year previously. He had enlisted the aid of his friend and persuaded him to give him an intravenous injection of the antibiotic. He remembered that the friend who had been in hospital had had to have an intravenous injection because it had a faster effect.

'An intravenous injection!' exclaimed Eddie involuntarily. He knew by this time that the Thai were capable of tackling anything, trained or not, but to dare to give an intravenous injection without knowing exactly how to do it was too much for Eddie to take quietly.

The friend held up the empty box which had contained the vial, and Eddie read the words on it with a rapidly sinking heart. The terramycin that had been injected was 'for intra-muscular use only'. The friend had duly located a blood vessel in the patient's arm, and pressed the plunger of the syringe to inject the terramycin. Unfortunately, he had injected into an artery, and not a vein. The terramycin instantly caused the blood in the artery to clot, causing severe pain. The patient had let out a yell of agony, waving his good arm while he held the painful arm stiffly before him. They tried one remedy after the other, but nothing alleviated the pain. Finally they had come to the hospital for help.

Eddie examined the arm. 'When did you give the injection?' he asked. 'Yesterday morning,' came the reply. Twenty-four hours ago! A day and a night for gangrene to develop. Would it be possible to reverse the process? Eddie arranged for immediate emergency surgery and excised the nerve centre in the patient's neck that was responsible for the continued spasm of the blood vessels. The next three days were full of tension for Eddie as he checked the patient's arm at regular intervals. Soon after the operation the pain had lessened appreciably, and the dark discolouration of the forearm receded. Eventually, only the tips of the fingers remained black and gangrenous. These tips eventually had to be amputated, but apart from that, the man's hand and arm had become normal again.

Eddie longed to get out of the hospital sometimes in order to evangelise the patients who had been treated and discharged. One of the missionaries at Manorom was Rowland Bell, whose work it was to visit patients once they had gone home, and he went out into the rice fields and the jungle every day, travelling everywhere by motorbike. It was Eddie's heartfelt wish to go out with Rowland one day a week. Imagine how elated he was when the hospital Superintendent, John Townsend, told him he was to be free of hospital duties each Thursday so that he could go out with Rowland.

One Thursday, while Eddie and Rowland were out on their motorbikes, they stopped at a simple coffee stall made of four posts with a roof of banana leaves. The woman at the stall had shown interest in the gospel on a previous visit, so Rowland talked to her again about Jesus Christ. As an illustration of what Jesus has done for sinners, he said to her, 'Say your son had committed murder and was sentenced to death, and say that someone came forward and offered to die in his place–'

But before he could continue, she interrupted, 'No, we wouldn't let it go that far! We would first find out what kind of murder my son had committed. Was it serious, very serious, or was it just an ordinary murder? And if it were an ordinary murder, we would then ask the police how much money was needed to prevent the case going to court. And if the murder was *very* serious, and the police could not simply cancel the docket, then we would ask them how much money they would need to postpone the trial to give our son an opportunity to cross the border and escape.' She absolutely could not understand Rowland's illustration.

After leaving the coffee stall they got on their motorbikes again and rode further into the countryside to look up a patient who had shown interest in the gospel while she had been in hospital, and who was now back at home. When

Eddie and Rowland eventually located this patient's home
– a crudely built hut on stilts and thatched with palm and
banana leaves – they were warmly welcomed and invited to
sit cross-legged on the floor with the parents of the patient.
The wife made some coffee, very sweet and strong, poured
in large amounts of sweetened condensed milk, and served
it to them with small glasses of jasmine Chinese tea so that
they could take a sip every now and then to refresh their
mouths. After an hour or so, Eddie and Rowland were invited to have lunch with the couple. It was not yet noon, but
they knew that the Thai did not have fixed times for meals.

'Go and catch a chicken so I can cook it for the meal,' the
wife told her husband.

Obediently he left the room and went down the steps to
the ground. Eddie could see him through the wide cracks
between the floorboards. Interested to see how the man
would catch the chicken, he watched intently. To his horror, he saw that all the chickens scratching in the dirt below
the house were diseased, with bald red and white eczema-
tous patches on their skin. His heart sank. How could he eat
such a bird? Thai cooking is very quick and it was not long
before Rowland was saying grace for the meal. While his
eyes were closed, Eddie was saying another, silent grace in
his heart as he asked the Lord to kill all germs in the food.
The Lord heard this prayer, because neither he nor Rowland
came to any harm after the meal that day.

Another day, Rowland and Eddie were walking in the
winding paths of the rainforest when they saw a woman
and a young girl coming towards them, walking hand in
hand. As they drew near, Eddie's gaze was drawn to the
daughter's face. Taking up most of the right side of her face

was a dark purple mass that pulled her mouth towards it. After a passing nod and brief greeting, the woman went on her way. Eddie, with his surgeon's training uppermost, quickly walked after her.

'You know, we can fix your daughter's face,' he assured her. 'I come from Manorom Hospital, and there we can operate on her. I cannot say we can make her beautiful, but I know that we can make her look much better than she does now.'

'*Plaaw!*' (Never!) came the strong negative reply. The woman started to turn away.

'If it is the thought of having to pay for the treatment, I want to tell you that we will do the operation for nothing!' Eddie said quickly, before the woman could leave.

'*Plaaw!*'

There was no mistaking the finality of that reply. Disconsolately, Eddie watched them disappear round a bend in the path. He turned to Rowland. 'Why won't she let me operate on her daughter?' he asked, disappointed.

'Well,' replied Rowland, 'if you'd been in Thailand as long as I have, you'd understand. It's because the people believe in reincarnation. The mother believes that the person whose spirit is now in her daughter's body was very bad in her previous life, and this deformity in the girl is her punishment. If the mother lets you operate on her daughter, she will never have any opportunity to make merit for her next reincarnated life. Her only hope is to bear the deformity patiently now – and then, maybe, she will be reborn as a normal person.'

Speechless, Eddie looked at his friend. The enormity of the harsh implications of the (seemingly harmless) belief in reincarnation suddenly became clear to him. From that time on, although he did not speak of it often, he kept this knowledge in his heart. With his new, deeper understanding of this aspect of Buddhism, he was better able to relate to his patients.

All doctors from other countries who want to work in Thailand long term must first pass a written and oral examination in the subjects they studied in their last four or five years at medical school. This examination takes three days. After some hectic swotting on Eddie's part (he has always been most conscientious), the appointed day finally arrived.

We joined the little crowd of examinees outside the Ministry of Health who were waiting for instructions before the start of the first paper. A tall, turbaned Sikh spoke excitedly to a group nearby, waving his arms animatedly. 'I have experience! I wrote the exam last year! I failed, but now I know what we should do! Listen to me, all of you! When you write the papers, take in as many different coloured pencils as you can, and use them to make your answers attractive. Rule lines! Draw diagrams! I don't believe the examiners read all the papers properly. You will see – you will pass!'

Another Westerner introduced himself to us while we waited in line. This was his second attempt, too, to pass the medical examination. Because he was a consultant physician we could not understand why he had not passed the basic examination. But then we learned that he intended to open a practice in Bangkok itself. We could see the hopelessness and disillusionment in his eyes as he spoke, as he knew very well that the Thai did not want foreigners opening competing practices in the city. (He did not pass the examination that time either.) Eddie and I gave an inward sigh of relief as we reminded ourselves that Manorom was rural, and had a shortage of medical doctors and nurses. This might help us to pass.

Once inside the building we sat at widely separated desks in a large room. When we had the papers before us I glanced hastily at mine – and sighed with relief. The questions were not in Thai, but in English. I relaxed, but not for long: it took almost as long to work out the meaning of each question as it did to write the answers. The third and final day of the examinations consisted of an oral. Each candidate in turn was taken into a room to face a panel of Thai specialists in all the major disciplines of medicine. Eddie was called before me. The time seemed to pass terribly slowly as I waited for him to emerge once more, but when he came out he seemed satisfied and relieved.

'How was it? Do you think you've passed?' I asked eagerly.

'I don't know. I hope so. But Dos, the doctor who asked me most of the questions, wasn't a surgeon at all, but a physiologist, and he asked me about the physiology of the kidney – the very stuff I revised!'

After a long wait my name was called. My heart was beating furiously and my cheeks were red with tension as I walked to the door. The panel of specialists spoke to me in hesitant English, but one of them, a psychiatrist, seemed much happier in Thai. When he found that I was willing to reply in Thai, the psychiatrist started to monopolise the questions. Eventually the oral examination became conversational, between the two of us, revolving around the problems attendant on treating mentally ill patients far upcountry where facilities for their treatment are few.

At last the examinations were over and we were free to

return to Manorom. Once back, we slipped easily into the routine work again and the days passed quickly. When we received a letter with the news that we had both passed the examination, it came as something of a surprise. We had almost forgotten about our ordeal by that time. At the end of the letter was a request that we send two photographs each of ourselves for our diplomas. Eddie still had several from the stock of photos that he kept for immigration requirements and he posted them the same day. Two days later we received another letter, also from the Ministry of Health. This letter was in Thai. It took us an hour with our huge Thai dictionary before we were able to make any sense out of it. Apparently the photographs that we had sent were totally unacceptable. First, our clothes were too casual for doctors in Thailand (Eddie had worn a short-sleeved, open-necked shirt, while I had on a sleeveless dress) and, second, we had both been smiling. The third reason why the photos had been rejected was that the pictures had been taken from an angle, and only one ear was visible.

The very next day we dressed more formally (how hot it was, too!) and went to Manorom market, where we took turns to face the photographer grimly, without a hint of a smile. As soon as we were out of the dark little shop Eddie peeled off his suit jacket and undid his tie. When he had also rolled up the sleeves of his long-sleeved shirt he started to look a bit more comfortable in the searing heat. While we were there in the village, Eddie posted the new photos. We did not expect to hear any more until our Thai medical diplomas arrived, but to our surprise we received a note by return of post, expressing satisfaction and gratification that our new photos were so much more suitable.

12

Christmas at Hua Hin

I will provide for you and your little ones.
(Genesis 50:21)

As parents, we appreciated the opportunity and privilege to have our children taught at OMF's school in Malaysia. Our three children at Chefoo slipped easily into the rhythm of being at school there for two long terms, broken by two seven-week-long holidays with us. While they were at school they were happy and kept busy, so began to get homesick only towards the end of each term. They had a long train journey of about 1,500 kilometres to and from Manorom, but this was exciting and not arduous for the children. (For the harassed teachers or dorm aunties who looked after them on the train, however, I am sure the journey was less exciting.) There were a large number of children going to join their parents in Thailand, so they almost filled an entire carriage. Imagine the excited, noisy children jabbering away, heads bobbing in and out of the windows while they nibbled from the snack-sized boxes of raisins that had been handed out to them when they boarded the train.

While the children were at Chefoo they were encouraged to write home each week, and were even given time in class to do this. These letters were a great encouragement to Eddie and me, as we felt the separation from our children very much. We also had regular letters and reports on their progress and well-being from their class teachers and the dorm aunties who were responsible for the children out of school hours and at night. All these teachers and dorm aunties were themselves missionaries, and they showed dedicated love and care for the children in their charge. They taught the children from the Bible (just as we used to do at home), and accompanied them to worship services in the school chapel each Sunday morning. Years later, long after their school days were over, all three vowed that the years spent at Chefoo were the very best of all. And that meant a great deal to us, as each of them attended various schools both before and after Chefoo.

Susan, only six years old, was placed in the dormitory for the younger girls. Although she never mentioned it in her letters, she was very homesick indeed. One evening, after the girls in the dorm had been settled in bed and the lights put out, she did not go to sleep for some time, but lay in her bed, tears falling silently. When the dorm auntie came back to check on her charges, she noticed that one of the other girls was crying into her pillow, overcome with homesickness.

'Can't you sleep, dear?' she asked gently and softly, so as not to wake the rest of the girls. In reply, the girl raised herself up and clung desperately to the older woman. 'Come with me and sit on my lap,' said the dorm auntie. 'I won't leave you alone to lie awake.' And she carried the little girl to the duty table in the centre of the dormitory. There, she cuddled and comforted the homesick girl until her eyes became heavy and started to close. Careful not to wake her, the dorm auntie carried her back to her bed and tenderly tucked her in. None of this was lost on Susan, homesick herself, and now feeling a little envious of the love and attention showered on her classmate.

The very next night, five minutes after the lights had been put out, Susan called to the dorm auntie, 'Please – I can't sleep!' To her deep disappointment, the reply she received was, 'Try for a little bit longer, Susan.' And before five more minutes had passed, Susan was fast asleep!

When Jenny was nine years old, she began to grasp the truth of salvation by faith in Jesus Christ and, in her usual enterprising manner, composed two choruses that illustrated that grasp of the essentials of the gospel message. The first chorus went like this:

> Why did He come to this poor world?
> Why did He come to this poor world?
> Can someone tell me why?
> Can someone tell me why?
> He came to save, His life He gave
> To rescue you and me.

And the second ran:

> Jesus is my Shepherd; I'm His little lamb.
> I'm going to love Him however I can.
> Jesus is my Saviour, died on Calvary's tree,
> Took away my sins and set me free.

In contrast with the regular communication we had from Chefoo School, we had not heard from David himself, nor had any news about him – either from the Home Director of OMF in South Africa, or from Christian friends there or even from the rector of the school or his wife, who were acting *in loco parentis* while we were away in Thailand. We comforted ourselves as best we could with the thought that 'no news is good news'. However, when we returned to South Africa for our first furlough (nowadays called 'home assignment') we were shocked to discover that David had not been at all happy or settled at the school. He had even run away three times. We realised that no one wanted to disturb us in our work, but we wished, nonetheless, that we had been told of this state of affairs.

When we had first been told that David would have to stay back in South Africa while the rest of the family went to the East, we knew that the separation would be extremely traumatic for him. The mission was adamant, however, because he was already ten years old and would only have been able to stay at Chefoo for one year. I do not think that either Eddie or I realised just how deeply painful the separation from the rest of his family had been for David. This emotional trauma plagued him for years – even when we stayed back in South Africa after that first furlough. We prayed much for wisdom from the Lord to know how to comfort him and to persuade him that we had not known anything about his emotional turmoil. He was totally convinced that we must have known all about his running away from the school, and yet had not loved him enough to do anything about it. He had not known that friends of ours had cared enough for him to collect sufficient money for him to spend his first long summer holiday in Thailand with us and the other children. Unfortunately, such a holiday for him was not possible, as in those days it was not usual for children and parents to be reunited from time to time as they are now. The OMF would not allow it, as they

feared that such a costly trip for David might create mis-
understanding among the general public or regular donors.

Ballet had always been one of Jennifer's great enthusi-
asms. During one holiday in Manorom, she was gripped
with the idea of producing a children's ballet. She was eager
to teach her younger sister Susan and her friend Janet
Townsend, the daughter of fellow doctors John and Ann
Townsend. To my consternation I was instructed to make
three tutus as quickly as possible. Desperately I searched the
linen cupboard, finding two rolls of mosquito netting, as yet
unused. Never before had I attempted such a challenge to
my dressmaking skills, and I was greatly relieved when my
three hastily made tutus proved acceptable to the girls.
After some weeks of concentrated practice sessions Jenny
announced that they were ready for the performance of the
ballet. The coming performance was made known around
the hospital compound by word of mouth, and over 40 missionaries and hospital staff members arrived at the hall at
the chosen time. The admission fee was only one baht,[1] and
Jenny announced that the total collected would be used as
a donation to the FEBC (Far Eastern Broadcasting Corpora-
tion) for its work of broadcasting gospel programmes to that
area of South-east Asia.

At the end of the short ballet, everyone clapped enthusi-
astically, faces beaming. Those sitting nearest to Eddie and
me waved their congratulations. No one had expected to
see a production of this quality from missionary children,
and no one had seen anything like it before at Manorom
Christian Hospital.

---

[1] At that time 20 baht was worth US$1, and 40 baht was worth £1.

By this time we had been in Manorom for nearly two years. We were making plans for our two-week holiday in December. We were fortunate that this holiday would fall over the Christmas and New Year festivities, as OMF reserved this desirable time for missionaries with young children. We were going to travel south to a delightful seaside holiday home kept by OMF where missionaries could stay without charge. Even our holiday rail fare was paid for by OMF. We were all excited at the prospect of seeing the sea again – it would bring back happy memories of holidays in South Africa, spent at the beautiful Garden Route town called Wilderness. We sat happily on our third-class slatted seats. A Thai lady who was sitting across from us pursed her lips and looked disapprovingly at me when the excited children climbed up on the wooden seats in order to see better out of the windows. Did I not know, she asked, that to put sandaled feet on the seat was a filthy habit and frowned on in Thailand?

The train stopped at almost every station and we were importuned by vendors of every conceivable type of foodstuff – from sticky rice steamed with black beans inside lengths of bamboo to barbecued chicken yellow with spices, soya bean milk and curries with coconut milk. Some vendors would board the train at a stop and march up and down the aisles with a filled tray while they called out their wares, leaving the train when their stocks were gone. As the train progressed south we looked out of the windows and feasted our eyes on the palms and luxuriant growth of the countryside. Roughly made dwellings with leafy roofs were common, each with a spirit house on a pedestal in the yard. To pass the time we had competitions to see who could spot the most spirit houses, but this proved impossible: there were too many and we lost count.

At last, after many hours, we saw the welcome sign 'Hua Hin' on the station as we came to our destination. We gathered our belongings, counted the children and stepped down into the harsh sunlight. We were glad to see that several bicycle trishaws were drawn up near the station to meet the train, as we needed two to take our bags and ourselves. Sitting behind the thin Thai man as he pedalled, we were amazed at how he could keep it up, sinewy legs pumping away with no apparent fatigue.

When we arrived at the holiday home, the children did not wait for us to pay the trishaw cyclist and gather our belongings. They ran down to the gleaming white sandy beach, removed their sandals and started to paddle in the water. This beach was very different from those we knew in South Africa, with gentle wavelets lapping at the shoreline. It was an ideal place for children, safe and shallow. While they played, Eddie and I were shown to our rooms in a separate block from the main house. The kitchen and dining area were also in a separate building. We unpacked quickly and joined the children on the beach.

It was glorious, staying at Hua Hin. The hostess there, Mrs Ruth Wilson, was warm hearted and a pleasure to get to know. The well-being of the missionaries holidaying there was first and foremost in her mind and nothing was too much trouble or too insignificant for her to do for her guests. The time slipped by smoothly, almost unnoticed, whole days being spent paddling and swimming in the warm, tropical water of the Gulf of Thailand and seeing who could build the highest sandcastle from the smooth, fine sand. Other missionary families invited our children to join them on fishing expeditions. They would hire a boat fitted with an outboard motor and fill it with children and a few parents to look after them, while the Thai man who owned the boat would steer it to a place where he knew there would be plenty of fish. He supplied tackle and bait for the children and showed them how to use it. It was an exultant, rowdy group of children who returned, standing up in the boat, holding up the brightly coloured, exotic fish they had caught. Eddie and I were sorry that we could not afford to return this hospitality. Ever since we had come to Thailand we had lived frugally on the basic quarterly allowance given to all missionaries. So far we had not been fortunate enough to receive any extra funds from supporters at home in South Africa, earmarked for our personal use. These other missionaries, however, were used to receiving personal gifts from their home countries from time to time.

Christmas Day was drawing nearer, and through the thin board partition between our room and theirs we could clearly hear the children's excited voices as they speculated on what presents they might receive.

'I'm going to get a doll that cries "Mama",' boasted Jennifer.

'And I'm going to get a toy train engine that really *goes*!' countered Anthony.

'But I don't know what I'll get!' wailed Susan. Then, 'But I'm sure I'll get something just as nice as your presents. . .'

As we listened to them our hearts sank. If, when they woke up on Christmas morning, they did not find the usual gaily wrapped parcels at the foot of their beds, they were bound to be bitterly disappointed. How could we explain to them that we had no spare funds in our account? How would they ever be able to understand just how much we longed to give them their hearts' desire?

Two days before Christmas Ruth called Eddie and me to the office in the main house. 'There's been an urgent telephone call from OMF HQ in Bangkok,' she told us. 'You two are needed there immediately.' We hurriedly made preparations, leaving the three children in the care of another missionary couple, and caught the first available train back to Bangkok. From the main station, Hua Lumpong, we took a trishaw to the entrance of the mission home compound in the narrow lane called Pan Road. In the office at the rear of the building we saw Brian Dean, who had summoned us from Hua Hin.

'Sorry to have brought you all the way back from your holiday,' he said. 'Will you please sign your names on these official forms? We've always signed on missionaries' behalf before, but suddenly the government is demanding original signatures.'

Just then Alma Cunningham, who worked in the office, caught sight of us and came across the room. 'What are you doing here?' she asked. 'I thought you were on holiday at Hua Hin!' We explained that we had been asked to return. 'Well, while you're here, let me go and get a letter that arrived for you yesterday from South Africa. I was on the point of readdressing it to Hua Hin.'

Tearing the envelope open eagerly, Eddie took out its contents. At once his eyes opened wide and he silently passed them to me. Inside were a cheque and a note from our church in Blanco, South Africa, explaining that the money was a personal gift for us for Christmas. We were stunned, then gradually began to realise what this gift would mean to us. First of all, we now had sufficient funds to buy Christmas gifts for our young family. Next, looking at the cheque, we saw that it could be drawn only on the Hong Kong and Shanghai Bank – and we realised that God had brought us to Bangkok where there was a branch of that bank just at the right time. Lastly, we just 'happened' to be in Bangkok on a Wednesday – the very day of the week that the Thrift Shop in the city was open! We sighed with gratitude as we understood what it meant to experience the Lord's provision. The right amount at the right time and in the right place.

After we had signed the official papers we caught a bus to the Thrift Shop in Raatchadamri Road in an upmarket area of Bangkok. Here, huge modern department stores vied for attention with luxurious tourist hotels and fashionable businesses. The Thrift Shop was at the end of a narrow lane off this road. At this shop used goods and clothing of good quality were donated, mostly from well-to-do businessmen and their wives stationed in Bangkok. Clothes were washed and ironed or dry-cleaned when necessary, and sold to the public at very reasonable prices. Here we could buy things usually of very good quality, at prices we could afford. The shelves and racks drew my eyes like a magnet and it was difficult to choose what to buy. At last we bought a toy for each child and had them wrapped in Christmas paper, and a small gift for both Eddie and me. We were pleased to find that there was still some money left. This would enable us to return some of the hospitality that had been so freely showered upon our family at Hua Hin.

In due course we caught a train back to Hua Hin, where we arrived tired but happy. The children were already in bed and asleep. We tiptoed into their bedroom and gently placed their presents at the foot of their beds, where they would be able to see them the moment they opened their eyes in the morning – Christmas Day.

That morning, Ruth Wilson organised a service of praise and worship in the large living room of the main building. The hot, humid air was alleviated to a certain extent by the slight movement of breeze that came through the wide-open windows on the seaward side of the room. Afterwards we all stayed on to sing carols. We adults sat in wicker chairs against the walls while the children sat cross-legged on the floor in front of us, facing the gaily decorated Christmas tree in one corner. The sparkling lights on the tree were reflected in their bright eyes. As we left for our own quarters, Ruth stood by the door, handing out to each woman missionary a gift she had made herself. So thoughtful, this dear lady had remembered that we missionaries had come from the much hotter, inland areas of Thailand and might feel cold near the coast, so she had knitted each of us a pair of pastel-coloured bed socks!

On Boxing Day we hired a fishing boat for 5 US dollars, inclusive of fishing lines and bait, and arranged for the owner to bring his boat to the shallow waters opposite the OMF holiday home. It was soon crammed full of excited children and some parents. After a full day on the water of the Gulf of Thailand they returned, proudly displaying the tropical fish they had caught.

All too soon our holiday came to an end and we found ourselves packing our suitcases again. We were all as brown as berries, rested and refreshed, and felt we could take on the world.

13

Health Hazard

And we know that all things work together for
good to those who love God.

(Romans 8:28)

During the early part of our third year at Manorom
recurrent attacks of vertigo, nausea and vomiting
began to interfere with my medical work. These
were due to Ménière's disease, relating to the inner ear and
the balance organ on the right side. The attacks were spo-
radic and in between them I was able to continue normally,
so I did not worry about them overmuch. Occasionally,
however, they were more severe. While I was examining
someone in the outpatients' department one morning, I
suddenly found the room whirling around me so much that
I could not stand any more, and lost my balance and fell to
the floor. I was extremely nauseous and had to keep my
eyes shut in order to avoid the vomiting that was brought
on by the spinning world around me. On that occasion I
was taken home on a trolley. I felt fine the next day, so carried on with my work.

Later that year we realised that Anthony was coming to the end of his time at Chefoo School and would need to continue his senior schooling back in South Africa. It was impossible for Eddie to leave his surgical work at the hospital, so I flew to South Africa with Anthony in order to make arrangements for him and David to continue their schooling there together. We wanted very much for them to be placed in a Christian school, and that meant a private school, but the schooling allowance given by OMF was only a fraction of the likely fee. In South Africa I spoke to Revd Molyneux, a member of the OMF Council in Cape Town. 'I know the perfect school for the boys!' he exclaimed. 'Michaelhouse, in Natal. The rector is a Christian and your boys will receive a first-rate education there.'

'What about their fees?'

'I'm sure they will be sympathetic,' he replied. 'You and Eddie are missionaries and I'm certain they'll understand.'

Michaelhouse College is over 1,000 kilometres from Cape Town, so the boys and I set out by car early one morning. The long drive was not without incident, as twice on the way I felt the warning signs of an imminent attack of vertigo. Thank God that He enabled me to stop the car on the verge both times before the dizziness became so acute that I could not press my foot hard enough on the brake. Looking back, I realise that it was extremely foolhardy to undertake that long drive in my condition, but in those days I had not fully understood just how disabling the symptoms of my Ménière's disease could be.

Once at the college we put our luggage in the house of the college chaplain, Revd Harold Clark, whose wife Rosemary was a very good friend of mine from school and university days. They had invited us to stay with them while we were visiting Michaelhouse. I was able to see the rector, Mr Rex Pennington, in his office at the college the next morning. I explained to him that we were missionaries in Thailand and that the school for missionaries' children did not provide secondary education, so our two sons were to continue their schooling in South Africa. I mentioned that Revd Molyneux had suggested that we try to place the boys at Michaelhouse and that he had thought we might be offered reduced fees on the grounds of our being missionaries.

'There is a slight difficulty,' said Rex. 'Our normal fees are high – over 1,000 rands per year for each boy. I understand that you and your husband are not members of the Church of the Province of South Africa. In almost all cases, the college board reduces fees only when parents are members of that Church.'

'But is that necessarily the case for us as missionaries?' I asked. 'The OMF gives us an allowance of only 360 rands per year for David, and 240 per year for Anthony.'

'I'll tell you what I'll do,' replied Rex. 'The board has a meeting this very afternoon. I'll put your case to them and see what they say. I'll come back to you after the meeting to tell you of their decision.'

That afternoon David, Anthony and I were in my bedroom. We prayed earnestly that the Lord would soften the hearts of the board members. We so waited on the Lord in our prayers that we were unaware of the passing of the hours until we heard a knock on the front door. It was the rector himself, come to tell us that the board had agreed unanimously to make an exception and to admit David and

Anthony to the school as boarders, with fees of only the small allowance given by OMF. The balance due on the fees would be made up later, on a deferred payment scheme, which would come into effect when we eventually returned permanently to South Africa. I really praised our heavenly Father that evening for His faithfulness and provision. Rosemary and Harold Clark gave their warm assurances that they would be there for the boys at all times, and would act *in loco parentis* in our absence. I left in good spirits to drive back to Cape Town next morning. I would stay in the OMF missionary home for some days before my return flight to Thailand.

I took the opportunity of a free morning to visit a friend, Moya Viljoen, who lived in the area of the Cape Town Gardens. After a few minutes of cheerful chatting, Moya left for the kitchen to make coffee. I rose from my chair to follow her, meaning to help her, when suddenly I was seized by such giddiness I could not stand. I collapsed on the floor, where I lay, my eyes shut against the extreme nausea that came over me whenever I dared open my eyes. That was how Moya discovered me when she returned with our coffee. Each time I ventured to open my eyelids a crack, the room would whirl about me crazily and I would want to vomit again. Hour after hour passed with no improvement. I was so wrapped up in my misery that I was unaware that Moya had telephoned for a doctor to come. Eventually I was able to drag myself to a bed, where I lay, too frightened to move.

By the time Professor Jarvis, Head of the ENT Department of Groote Schuur Hospital, arrived at the house, the attack had lasted for five hours. Fortunately, the dizziness and nausea were lessening by then. After examining me, Professor Jarvis told me that this severe attack meant I could wait no longer. I needed urgent surgery for my Ménière's disease. He said that in King's College Hospital in London a relatively new procedure involving ultrasound was being followed, and that I should go to England to be treated. He arranged by telex for my urgent admission. Little did I know at that time that I was to be only the sixty-sixth person in the world to be treated in that way. The next day I cabled Eddie in Thailand to tell him of the proposed surgery and ultrasound treatment. I felt he had the right to know, as the surgery was to be near the brain. Then I booked my flight to London and back. But how was I able to pay for this unexpected expense? Let me tell you how our heavenly Father met that need, even before the need had arisen.

Years before, while Eddie and I were still in Thaba 'Nchu, we learned that Norman, my oldest brother, was in desperate straits. From being governing director of his firm, he had been forced into demotion by majority shareholders. He felt he could not accept the inferior position of managing director, subject to every whim of this shareholder lobby, and so he resigned. He wanted to start a new company and needed capital to do so. Eddie and I took out all the money we had in our joint bank account and lent it to him; he undertook to repay the loan when he was in a position to do so. For some years after that, I received an annual token amount of money as a non-executive director of his new firm, while he was still building up the company. All of a sudden, out of the blue, while I was in South Africa doing my best to find a suitable school for David and Anthony, a cheque from

Norman arrived for me at the OMF mission home. It was certainly not a mere token amount this time – it was for 1,000 rands! I found to my delight that it was more than enough to pay for my airfare to Britain and back, with money left over.

While I was packing in preparation to fly to London, Eddie, in faraway Thailand, had decided that if I were to have the operation in London, he should be at my side. He could not possibly have afforded an air ticket from Bangkok to London, except that he, too, had been the unexpected recipient of God's provision – again, like me, before the need had arisen. Two years earlier, Christian Pabel, who was a missionary with another organisation, had told Eddie that he wanted to give him some money. When he first heard this, Eddie refused the gift, saying that we had all we needed. The same thing happened the next year too. But in the third year, Christian told Eddie that this time he would not accept a refusal. He was convinced that the Lord wanted him to give money to Eddie. He said that although the money was not then available, it would be ready in some months' time. And so, in due course, Christian gave Eddie the promised cheque. Only a short time after that my cable arrived. Now Eddie had enough money for a single airfare to London.

Following the advice of a missionary colleague, Eddie left Manorom for Bangkok with a small bag containing a change of underclothes, pyjamas and his toiletries, just in case he was fortunate enough to get an immediate flight. Well, even then, the Lord was making his pathway smooth: a charter flight had a single seat still available. Under normal circumstances, Eddie could not possibly have completed the necessary paperwork (tax clearance certificate, and so on) in time before the plane's scheduled departure. When Eddie returned to the mission home from the tax office, however, he was greeted by Arnold Melbourne, who excitedly called to him to hurry. The plane had been delayed by two hours, so it was still possible for Eddie to get to the airport in time.

The wonderful provision of the Lord was not yet over. When Eddie reached London he went by bus straight to OMF Headquarters in Newington Green, where he was made welcome. After a good night's sleep he was up early the next morning, as he felt an inner urge to get to Heathrow in time to meet the South African Airways plane that was due later that morning. When he arrived at Heathrow the plane had just landed. Patiently, he waited in Arrivals with scores of other people, hoping with all his heart that he had met the right plane. And he had. His heart leapt when he caught sight of me. Incredible as it seems, I had not a thought as to what I should do next. Without knowing that Eddie would be there to meet me and guide me, I caught sight of his dear face as he waited for me. It felt so *right* to see him there! I shall never forget the thrill it gave me to see Eddie's smiling face. It was an unforgettable experience of God's kindness, love and care, as fresh in my memory today as if it had happened yesterday.

Eddie took me back with him to OMF at Newington Green. Because we were both in light cotton clothes with short sleeves, most unsuitable for the cold weather of early March, we were given the address of a branch of the Plymouth Brethren fairly nearby. They would supply us with warm clothes, the hostess at Newington Green told us. We found the Brethren's offices easily and were welcomed warmly and kindly. Generously, they gave us all that we could possibly need. Among Eddie's gifts was a luxurious, warm Harris tweed suit, and I was given nightwear, a bed jacket and a hot-water bottle for my upcoming stay in hospital, as well as a beautiful warm coat. We were overwhelmed by their kindness.

When I had been admitted to King's College Hospital, I lay rigid in my bed, frozen with cold. The ward's heating had been switched off the previous day and the tremendous change from summer heat in South Africa to the chill of early spring in England had left me shivering uncontrollably as I lay under a single, light, summer-weight blanket. I had forgotten it was possible to feel so cold! But a kind nurse from Jamaica noticed my predicament and asked the ward sister to turn the heating back on, and soon I could relax once again. The surgeon, anaesthetist and nurses were all most kind, and the operation took place without a hitch. Afterwards I had to take part in exercises to retrain my brain, as the balance organ on the right side had been destroyed during the surgery. The exercises were aimed at helping me to walk normally without overbalancing. Within a few months of the operation my right ear became completely and utterly deaf; the auditory nerve on that side had died as a result of the ultrasound therapy. I did not mind the unilateral deafness, however, as my vertigo, nausea and vomiting had disappeared for ever.

While Eddie was at Newington Green and I was in hospital, David and Dorothy Watts, two old friends in north Wales, generously provided a car for Eddie to use. This saved him from having to take three buses each day as he visited me. On my discharge from hospital, the car was to be ours to use until the time came for us to leave Britain. I was all right – I had my return air ticket to South Africa and from there to Bangkok, but Eddie had only been able to buy a single ticket to London, and still had to get back to Thailand somehow. When we inquired about the price of a single airfare from Heathrow to Bangkok, we found to our astonishment that the money left over from paying for my fare was just a little bit more than was needed to pay for Eddie's ticket. Our Lord had, once again, supplied our every need, even before we realised that the need would arise.

14

Time Out

Come now . . . and I will send you.
(Exodus 3:10)

On our return to South Africa for our first furlough
(or home assignment, as it is called nowadays) we
were thrust immediately into a round of deputation meetings, speaking engagements and participation in
the monthly OMF prayer meetings in the Cape Town area.
The two girls stayed with us in the mission home, while the
boys were at their boarding school in Natal.

On the evening of our final deputation meeting, just
before we were to speak, we were given an unexpected letter from the General Director of OMF. What a shock we had
when we read it! In his letter, the Director proposed that we
stay back in South Africa for a time in order to care and provide stability for our children, as they would not be returning to the East with us, but would stay in South Africa for
their further schooling. We knew that David especially had
been traumatised by the years he had to spend alone in
South Africa, but our being back on furlough had already

made a big difference to his disquiet. Because we had given absolutely everything – house, furniture, washing machine, and so on – to the Lord in order to obey His call to missionary service, this new development meant a completely new start as we readjusted to life in South Africa once more. At first, the prospect seemed extremely daunting. Later, however, we realised how very wise this decision had been. We would be at hand during our children's potentially stormy teenage years and, especially, would be able to reassure David that we loved him and would never forsake him.

First, we had to find a place to live. As it happened, in God's providence, I received an invitation at that very time from a fellow anaesthetist with whom I had worked in Groote Schuur Hospital before we went to Thailand. He asked me to come and work in George Hospital, as there was a need there for more anaesthetists. We knew the picturesque town of George, situated in a lovely coastal area called the Garden Route, and we were both eager to go there. But where were we to find a house that we could afford? After searching desperately, we found a little house just large enough to take the whole family at a squeeze, the deposit taking every penny we had invested in a unit trust fund years before. We named the house 'Sririchaa', after a town on a beautiful beach off the Gulf of Thailand. We had once been given a short island holiday there by the Danish firm Dumex of the East Asia Trading Company. It had been a gesture of gratitude to Eddie, who had helped them by distributing clothing among the poor in Central Thailand when Danish missionary Peder Jorgensen had returned to Denmark after appointing Eddie as his successor in the work.

Now we had to find some furniture somehow, though we

had no money left after paying the deposit on the house. Once again, the Lord was very good to us. The Christian owner of a furniture store in George offered us the use of basic furniture free of charge for six months. (He even told us that if after the six months we did not want to buy the items we had borrowed, we could simply return them to him. Of course we did no such thing!) Next, Eddie needed to find full-time work. He learned that the surgeon attached to the provincial hospital at George was soon to leave to take up a post in Saudi Arabia. Eddie applied for this post and was successful.

I learned a great deal about managing on a shoestring during those first years of being back in South Africa. The children were at boarding schools, so there were only the two of us to cater for except during school holidays. I bought fruit and vegetables from a wholesaler in the town, selecting trays of older or bruised fruits because they were cheaper. I remember buying a whole box of rather overripe tomatoes at a time, as they were really cheap, and then setting to in the kitchen to make tomato soup, tomato sauce, tomato jam and tomato *bredie*[1] as quickly as I could, before the tomatoes became unusable.

With David already settled in Michaelhouse, we had arranged for Anthony to be admitted as a boarder to Cord-wallis, the preparatory 'feeder' school for Michaelhouse. We enrolled the two girls at the nearby Collegiate Girls' School, also as boarders. By this arrangement, the four children were able to travel together each time they came home on holiday and when they returned to school. The

---

[1] A slowly cooked stew.

only disadvantage was that George was not near the route of the main railway line from Natal, so Eddie had to drive 240 kilometres to Beaufort West in the arid Karroo to meet their train at the start of each holiday, and drive them back to Beaufort West to catch the train when they returned to their schools.

Eddie was often called out at night for surgical emergencies in addition to his day-time duties. He found that he adapted quickly to the imperious summons of the telephone, making split-second decisions that were often essential for the survival of a desperately ill patient, while he was brought by speeding ambulance from his home. Although he did not enjoy the interruptions to his slumber, Eddie found that the drama of each emergency brought him energy and alertness to counteract his fatigue.

Once he was telephoned at midnight by a doctor at a hospital in a nearby town about a man who was on the point of death, with a gaping machete wound in his chest. The doctor was at his wits' end. Eddie rattled off a stream of urgent instructions for the patient's resuscitation, as his blood pressure had fallen alarmingly. He then dressed, got into his car and sped to the town. His speed alerted traffic policemen, whom he recruited to clear the road before him. When he saw the patient's poor condition, however, his heart sank. The case seemed hopeless – the hospital did not have the facilities for the type of drastic surgery needed. As emergency first aid treatment Eddie simply undergirded the heart to the breastbone to lessen the constant haemorrhage, so that the intravenous fluid might have a chance of restoring the patient's blood pressure sufficiently. He told the young doctor that if the patient was still alive after an hour, he was to send him by ambulance to George Hospital, where Eddie would be waiting.

In his heart, Eddie was doubtful that the patient would survive. Nevertheless, he drove back to George Hospital, where he summoned the anaesthetist on call and mobilised the theatre staff, warning them of the coming emergency and asking them to prepare the operating theatre without delay. Still, in his heart, he could not help wondering if the patient would survive long enough to get to George. It was quite a shock to him when he actually heard the ambulance's siren as it drove up to the casualty entrance. The driver and attendant paramedic quickly got the patient out and onto a hospital trolley. Without any delay, waiting porters pushed the trolley into the operating theatre.

Because the patient was unconscious, it was not necessary to give him any anaesthetic. Instead, the anaesthetist administered pure oxygen in an attempt to help resuscitate the collapsed and dying man. When Eddie made his first incision he found that the patient's blood pressure was so low that there was no bleeding from skin or muscles. He was horrified to find that the massive chest wound had severed the blood vessels between the lung and the heart and had also sliced open the paper-thin covering of the heart. The heart had stopped all normal contractions and was simply rotating very slowly in its dying state. Hastily Eddie sutured all the severed blood vessels. As soon as these were sutured, the heart's normal contractions returned, the blood pressure began to rise and the superficial vessels started to bleed and had to be controlled. As he worked, Eddie wondered if the patient could ever survive this dreadful ordeal. In the ward where the patient was taken after the surgery, Eddie gave detailed instructions to the nurse in charge. With a prayer on his lips, he returned home. It was then 4 a.m.

At 7 o'clock the next morning Eddie drove to the hospital and went straight to check on his night-time patient. As he entered the ward he found it in confusion. The ward sister was extremely flustered. Eddie's 19-year-old patient, who had almost died the night before, was sitting up in his bed, angrily demanding to have breakfast, and would not be pacified!

As soon as we were settled, I started to work part-time, giving anaesthetics for a surgeon and also for three dentists. The dental anaesthetics were short and light, so they took place in the dental surgeries. Appointments were made for several children at a time (they were generally between five and eight years old), for extractions of milk teeth. I enjoyed spending time with the children before the start of the session, gaining their trust and demonstrating to them how they could 'blow their own teeth right'. By using the technique of encouraging them to breathe strongly in and out through their mouths, I made them believe that this action of theirs would actually result in correction of their dental decay. If they somehow felt they remained in control, and were not going to be at the mercy of a strange adult doctor, I hoped they would not be so likely to panic or be terrified. By the time I introduced a potent anaesthetic agent into the air/oxygen that they were breathing in and out, they were already fairly dizzy from the hyperpnoea (excessive respiration) and were unaware of the smell and effect of the anaesthetic agent.

As each child came into the dental surgery, I would be waiting there alone, so I could gain the small patient's trust, having sent the dentist himself and his assistant out until the child was anaesthetised. Of course, nowadays such a practice is frowned upon. But in the four or five years during which I anaesthetised almost 5,000 children in this simple manner for minor dental procedures, I did not meet any hitch, and no child was traumatised or suffered any harm.

Each time our four children came home for holidays, I was careful to get up early enough in the morning to do all the household chores, washing, ironing and cooking before they were up and dressed. I did not want to be seen by them as a mother who was always busy around the house – one who did not really care much about them. I wanted to counter any emotional trauma or underlying insecurity that might be in them by being available for them during their waking hours. And so the children grew closer to Eddie and me and more secure in their home. We often played word games or went swimming together. For me it proved to be really worthwhile to get up so early – the disadvantage of losing some sleep was more than outweighed by the memorable hours we spent together as a complete family.

When we had been back in South Africa for almost a year, Eddie reminded me that our permanent residence visas for Thailand would soon be due for their annual renewal. (If we did not report to the immigration department in Bangkok in time, we would automatically lose these visas, and would then possibly not be able to return to Thailand in the future.) What could we do? We had no spare money for airfares. Yet we felt under a compulsion to return. So we prayed earnestly for wisdom and guidance from the Lord if He wanted us to work in Thailand again at a later date. In the meantime we found information about a cheap, short tour to the Far East – two days in Hong Kong and two days in Thailand. Eddie booked provisionally for the tour, even though we did not have the money to pay the fares.

One day we received an invitation to visit a couple whom we did not know very well, and went to their home in the Wilderness, a few miles outside George. These two elderly people were devout Christians and we had a good time of warm fellowship with them. We did not mention a word to them regarding our dilemma about the visas. Yet God answered our prayers in a way we could not have imagined. As we stood outside their seaside home, shaking hands in farewell, I was given an envelope, after which my hand was clasped meaningfully. When we returned home and examined the envelope, we found it contained a cheque made out to us – and the amount was a little more than we needed to pay our fares for the Far East tour. The Lord knew, of course, that we had no money of our own for these fares and had provided sufficient for us, with 20 rands left over for incidental expenses that arose on the way.

The next year, as the time to renew our visas drew near, we were again given some money unexpectedly. This time it was not enough to pay for our fares completely: the Lord knew that by then we had saved some money towards that purpose. By the end of the fourth year, however, we received no gift of money. The Lord knew, of course, that now we could afford the fares ourselves. Year after year, we went faithfully to renew our resident visas, looking to the future when once again we would be able to return to the work to which God had called us in Thailand. Other missionaries whom we saw in Bangkok while we were on this errand were a little incredulous at our persistence. Even though we were not sure exactly when we would be able to work in Thailand again, we simply continued to renew our visas because of an inner conviction that God would call us back when His time was right.

As the years passed, Eddie started up a private surgical practice in our old home town of Oudtshoorn, an hour's drive away. From time to time he asked me to give anaesthetics there too, as well as my work in George. I remember one afternoon very well, when I had been called urgently to Oudtshoorn because of an emergency. A young man, riding on his 1,000cc Kawasaki motorbike, had skidded at a turn, and when his bike hit the barrier at the side of the road he had been flung some distance in the air, sustaining severe injuries to his leg. When I had changed quickly into cap, gown and boots, I entered the theatre. There, on the floor alongside the operating table, was the patient, lying on a canvas stretcher cover. He was bleeding profusely from his mutilated leg, with the skin of the leg wrenched off like a stocking, lying on the floor beyond his foot.

Eddie decided that I should anaesthetise the patient while he lay on the floor so that he could first scrub the leg with soap and water to clean it from the debris of leaves, stones and dirt. First Eddie used soap and water, followed by saline solution and finally Betadine (an iodine compound). During this time I crouched alongside the patient's head as I monitored his condition under anaesthesia. After the washing and cleaning was finished, Eddie, the theatre sister and assistant nurse scrubbed up again and put on fresh sterile gowns and gloves. For two hours Eddie worked on this leg, painstakingly restoring things to as normal a position as possible.

Some time later, Eddie decided to send the patient for specialised after-treatment, because Oudtshoorn Hospital did not have the advanced facilities needed to immobilise the leg with the comminuted fractured bone and damaged muscles and skin. When the patient first arrived at the teaching hospital in Cape Town, he was told that his leg would need to be amputated. 'Oh no you don't!' he objected strongly. 'Dr Rose in Oudtshoorn told me that my leg could get better without amputation.' And his faith in Eddie's judgement proved correct. A few years later I met him, walking with a stick, but still possessing both his legs.

Our earnings increased bit by bit and we found we could afford to move to a larger house. When we made an offer for this house, it was less than the percentage down payment normally required but we would not have enough money to pay for transfer of the property into our names, and we had no more cash available. I told the attorney, Mr Solly Miller, that we had prayed about making this offer and felt at peace about it. The company offering the house for sale later went bankrupt and the bank seized all the properties it owned in various parts of South Africa. Because we had not taken transfer, our new home was now at risk of being seized with the rest. Imagine how we felt when we learned that our home was one of only two properties in South Africa that the Supreme Court in Johannesburg had allowed to be released for sale! As Solly told Eddie, 'Your prayers have been answered.'

By this time we had been back in South Africa for almost nine years and the children had all left school. We were almost losing hope that we would be able to return to Thailand and continue our missionary work. We doggedly continued to renew our resident visas each year, however, not wanting to lose these precious stamps in our passports. One day, as I was reading my Bible, in Matthew 20 I came to the parable of the landowner who hired men to work in his vineyard. He hired them at different times throughout the day, right up to 'the eleventh hour'. The thought kept coming into my mind that even though we might not have very many years left in which to serve the Lord in Thailand, we would be like the labourers who were hired last. Even though the hour was late and there were not many hours left to work, those labourers were still hired. I felt a new resolve. Whatever might happen, I would be ready.

When we returned to Thailand for the tenth (and, as it turned out, final) time, the official at the immigration department in Bangkok informed us that we would require new books for our resident visas. He said that they would be ready in two weeks' time. As this was Tuesday and our return flights were scheduled for Saturday evening, we expostulated politely in Thai, only to meet stony indifference. We returned to the mission home and told Arnold Melbourne, the OMF secretary, about this new development. He told us to return to the immigration department immediately, taking our air tickets with us so that we could explain about the date of our return flights. The official concerned simply stated that we should return on Friday at 1 o'clock in the afternoon. Our hearts sank, as our tour flight was due to leave in the evening of the next day, Saturday. Could everything be done within the few hours left on Friday afternoon? With rather heavy hearts we returned to the OMF mission home to wait out the specified period.

On Friday at the appointed time we presented ourselves again and were grateful to be given pristine new books without undue delay. By that time, however, it was already 4 p.m. Imagine the turmoil in our hearts as we anticipated trying to get a tax exemption certificate signed by a government official at that time on a Friday afternoon! As soon as we had left the building we crossed the street in search of a taxi to take us to the Inland Revenue department. Even though our financial position was below the threshold for paying income tax, all residents of Thailand were obliged to show a tax clearance certificate before they were allowed to leave the country. The next hour would be crucial for us. Bangkok, a sprawling city, had a population of 6 million at that time and we were planning to drive from one end of it to the other during the late afternoon rush hour.

We found a taxi fairly easily and told the driver of our destination, asking him to please hurry, as we had to get there before 5 o'clock, or the department would be closed. Once again we were given a demonstration of God's love and power. Our driver did not follow main roads but took small roads and lanes, all nearly empty of traffic, and got us there in time. In the building in which we were to ask for the tax clearance certificates we found a senior official who was most kind and efficient too. On the other side of the huge, hangar-like room filled with open-plan offices, she pointed out a lady dressed in green silk who would be able to help us. All went well and by 5 o'clock that afternoon we were back at the mission home. As we walked up the driveway we met Arnold Melbourne and told him what had happened. He was amazed. 'This is a miracle!' he said. 'The Lord must definitely want you back here – the usual time taken for a missionary to get a new book, tax clearance certificate and then the new visa is about two weeks!'

Only a few months after that adventure we received an invitation from Thailand to return. This invitation was to return as 'partners of OMF' in a professional capacity as lecturers in the Faculty of Medicine at the Prince of Songkhla University in Hat Yai, South Thailand. The invitation had come from *Acharn*[2] Krassenai, the Vice Dean, who was a Christian.

We accepted the invitation. David had got a post with the merchant navy group Safmarine, Anthony was in his first year at the University of Cape Town, studying psychology, and Jenny had been accepted to study for a diploma in ballet at the UCT Ballet School. Susan, who had started training as a nurse in Groote Schuur Hospital in Cape Town, decided that she would rather continue her training in the UK. Because Eddie had arranged to attend a surgical conference there, she asked him to see if he could arrange for her to train there during his visit. Wonderfully, by God's help, in spite of thousands of applications for only 40 posts, he was able to get her into the Glasgow Royal Infirmary.

And so, free of home ties and responsibilities, we sold our home and furniture once again, giving some of our furniture and our new washing machine to the OMF mission home. Within an incredibly short space of time, we were sitting in a Boeing 747, winging our way back to our beloved Thailand.

---

[2] A title of respect, given to teachers, ministers, doctors, pastors, etc.

15

Students in Hat Yai

Fear not, for I am with you.
(Isaiah 43:5)

Working at the Prince of Songkhla University
was a tremendous change from being in Manorom at the OMF mission hospital. Instead of
being among other Western missionaries, living in a simple
wooden house on stilts within a compound surrounded by
rice paddies, we found ourselves almost the only Westerners
among hundreds of Thai, in a very large, modern university
with many multi-storey concrete buildings on an extensive
campus that was set in the big, bustling city of Hat Yai. We
found we were to stay in one of the modern, three-room
flats that had been built to accommodate doctors and their
families who were lecturers in the Faculty of Medicine. As
we explored our new home we were agreeably surprised to
find that the lounge and main bedroom were fitted with air
conditioners, and that these worked efficiently. The bathroom was tiled and had a proper built-in shower and a
Western-style toilet. There was even a washing machine! I
did not even mind that it had been installed on one side of

the entrance lobby, near the front door of the flat. At first we were rather overwhelmed by all these amenities, but in next to no time we took them for granted.

We soon found that the seasons in the southernmost provinces of Thailand are very different from those in Central Thailand. Here, it was *always* swelteringly hot; the temperature was 38°C or more in the day, and even at night it was never less than 30°C. The humidity, too, was unbearable and all university buildings were air-conditioned. We found that the heavy monsoon rains started a month or two earlier and lasted longer – often for up to five months – and floods in the streets occurred annually. We soon accepted air conditioning as a necessity rather than a luxury.

The Southern Thai dialect was incomprehensible to us at first, with some of its tones opposite to those used in Central Thailand, and with clipped words spoken at such a speed that it was like a machine gun firing. In Central Thailand the language was classical Thai – like Oxford English – while in the South the dialect was so broad as to be unintelligible to us. Only when we had been living in Hat Yai for some months were we able to grasp the meaning of what had been said. There is a favourite story told in South Thailand that illustrates the rapid-fire characteristics of the Southern Thai dialect. It is told with pride. Two passengers, both from South Thailand, were sitting in trains going in opposite directions, each looking out of the window. The trains passed each other at speed, and even in that instant of passing, the two passengers were able to exchange remarks with each other. The first man asked a question, *'Nye?'* And the passenger in the other train managed to reply, *'Yai!'* Translated, this means that the first man asked the second man, 'Where are you going?' and the second man replied that he was going to Hat Yai.

Eddie and I started work in the Medical Faculty – Eddie in the Department of Surgery with 17 other surgeons, and I in the Department of Anaesthetics. Right at the beginning we were told that this was a Buddhist university. We were warned very solemnly not to speak openly to others about Christianity. Our hearts sank. Should we do so, we would be expelled from the university with immediate effect. What a difference from the absolute freedom to speak about the Lord that we had enjoyed in Manorom! But then, surprisingly, we were told that if a Thai should ask a question about our faith, we could answer freely. We also found out that while we were in the confines of our own flat we could speak about Christianity without restraint.

One day shortly after we had started work, I was in the Medical School canteen, choosing my lunch. A young nurse who worked with anaesthetists in theatre sat down at my table as I arrived with my tray. I recognised her as Kaysinee, and greeted her in Thai. Then I bowed my head and shut my eyes to thank the Lord for the food before me.

'Are you ill, *Acharn*?' she asked with concern.

'No, Kaysinee, I'm a Christian, and I'm thanking God for my food,' I replied.

'So you're a Christian,' she said. 'I've always wanted to be a Christian!'

Unfortunately, after such a promising beginning, I soon realised that her statement was made simply out of politeness to me, and she had not the remotest intention of ever becoming a Christian.

Eddie's work in the Department of Surgery was often

made more difficult by the fact that in the early days he could not understand all that his fellow surgeons were saying. They would rattle off clipped words in Southern Thai, not caring whether he could follow their meaning or not. At the beginning of each day, they stood in a group waiting for Professor Prasert to join them, and then suddenly wheeled about and disappeared into a nearby lift. Eddie was often left looking at their departing backs, and then faced the task of searching the many surgical wards in the faculty building before he could find and join them.

His work included teaching medical students at the bedside of patients as well as undertaking lectures and surgical operations. One day, as he stood with two medical students beside the bed of a man who had been extremely ill with acute inflammation of his gall bladder, a young Thai surgeon overheard Eddie tell the students that in this patient's case, because he was improving, conservative treatment was indicated. This would enable the surrounding swelling and delicate inflamed tissue to recover. Surgery could then be performed two months later, he said, and this would be both easier and safer. Suddenly the young Thai surgeon intervened. 'Don't listen to him!' he cautioned the students urgently. 'We believe that the treatment for acute gall bladder inflammation should always be immediate surgery!' Eddie withdrew, embarrassed at this outburst in front of both the patient and the students. He had been reminded that not all schools of surgery teach the same methods of treatment.

Eddie was very frustrated by the gagging order from the authorities. He longed to tell the Thai about the good news of the gospel. All his adult life he has been eager to speak for the Lord. He reminds me of what the prophet Jeremiah wrote: 'His word was in my heart like a burning fire shut up in my bones; I was weary of holding it back, and I could not' (Jeremiah 20:9). Imagine Eddie's joy when he found out that he would be permitted to speak to any seriously ill or dying patient. The university authorities regarded this as 'comfort to the dying'.

For my part, giving anaesthetics in the university hospital was also a new experience. Instead of having an anaesthetic nurse ready to place in my hand the syringes I had already filled, I found I had to cope with the whole procedure on my own – putting up an intravenous drip, giving an intravenous injection, and introducing an endotracheal tube into the patient's throat to ensure adequate respiratory support while the respiratory muscles were paralysed during abdominal surgery. I felt I needed at least one more hand! New also was having to keep the surgeon and theatre staff waiting until a small child gave permission for the anaesthetic. Once the entire theatre staff waited from early morning until mid-afternoon before a four-year-old girl agreed to allow the anaesthetist to administer the anaesthetic so the planned surgery could proceed.

Compared with the stress involved in our clinical work, giving lectures was much more fun. Eddie and I both found that the ethnic Chinese students were most industrious, spending time in the Medical School library and reading everything they could get their hands on. Not so pleasant was one result of this energy – their habit of producing extremely difficult questions for us to answer! The Thai students, on the other hand, were pleasant and more easy going. Regrettably, this relaxed attitude caused quite a few students to ask us regularly about the questions that were to be put to them in a future examination paper. Needless to say, we did not enlighten them.

One day we were invited to attend a conference for new lecturers. Eddie and I were the only Westerners present. The speaker asked if there were any in his audience who had ever smacked or disciplined their own children. Eddie and I were the only two who had ever done this, and all eyes were on us as our hands went up, lonely in the crowd. Then the speaker went on to teach us how to reply to students who gave incorrect answers. 'If a student gives the wrong answer,' he said, 'whatever you do, don't tell him he's wrong! That would cause him to feel ignorant. Rather reply to him like this: "Very good. But have you thought of this?" and then you should tell him the correct answer.' This was an entirely new concept to us. We had been brought up to recognise a reply as either right or wrong, with no middle road. This conference was an eye-opener to us and was a great help in enabling us to adapt our approach to the Thai students.

It was a joy to meet Apithan and Mong, two Christian medical students in their fourth and third year of study respectively. They came to our flat to introduce themselves to us. Apithan was the only believer in his entire family, while Mong, a charming young woman, had been brought up in a Christian home. They were the only ones in their classes who were not Buddhist, and it was not easy for them to be faithful to their beliefs in those surroundings. Apithan confided in us that for four years, ever since he had begun his training in that university, he had been praying earnestly that the Lord would send a Christian lecturer. And now his prayers had been answered generously – instead of one Christian lecturer, the Lord had sent two! After that first meeting, it became their habit to come to us one evening each week. Gradually this became a weekly 'cell group' of student believers from all the different faculties of the university. Although this cell group began with a few, by the end of three years there were 35 regular attendees.

One evening Apithan came to us alone and confided that he was in love with Mong. Unfortunately for him, he knew that a consultant gynaecologist was wooing Mong. How could Apithan, a mere fellow student, compete? He was despondent. Then, not long after that, he came to see us again, his face lightened and at peace. He told us how he had been rereading the book of Ruth, and when he came to the story of Ruth and Boaz, he had been really touched by the way Boaz, in love with Ruth himself, had given the nearer kinsman-redeemer first place, in offering him the opportunity to marry Ruth. Apithan saw himself as a Boaz, and the consultant as the kinsman-redeemer. He was relieved of his stress and tension by leaving the whole matter in God's hands. When, eventually, the Lord brought him and Mong together as husband and wife, we rejoiced with them both. Now, years later, their home in Bangkok is a place of witness to the faithfulness of God and their three children are being brought up to know the Lord.

When we first knew him, Apithan was the only member of his family to be a Christian. Next to come to the Lord was his brother, followed by his mother, Mrs Buasri. His father, Mr Puang, an extremely wealthy businessman, is no longer antagonistic to the gospel, and Apithan is looking forward to the day when he will accept the salvation there is for him in Jesus Christ.

Towards the end of our first year at the university, Eddie received a call for help from our elder son, David, in South Africa. He had been detained for taking an anti-government stand in Cape Town. Eddie's immediate wish was to fly to South Africa himself to see how he could help. Unfortunately, we did not have enough money for that flight. Eddie asked the OMF Field Director, but was told that to lend money to a missionary for this purpose was not in accordance with OMF policy. His disappointment was crushing, even though he understood the rationale behind this decision. So we prayed.

One day not much later, a letter arrived from South Africa for Eddie from his erstwhile receptionist in Oudtshoorn. In it she enclosed a bank draft, explaining that the fee for an operation Eddie had performed on a workman injured on duty seven or eight years previously had just been paid! Wonderfully, this bank draft was just sufficient to pay for a return flight to South Africa. So, once again, we knew the provision of the Lord. Eddie flew to South Africa and was able to pay for David's legal expenses and personal needs. When the case against him was heard and David's background and friends had been gone into, he was told that he had been very foolish, and was cautioned, fined and discharged.

While Eddie was away I had the dubious pleasure of experiencing our first rainy season in South Thailand. Now I realised why the blocks of flats in the university had been built on stout cement pillars. Water lapped at these pillars hungrily, but could not reach the level of the flats themselves. There were no cars parked under the flats any more. They had been moved to higher ground, almost half a kilometre away. With the floodwaters now ankle deep, we had to remove our shoes or sandals before we could climb the stairs to the flats. In the mornings, before the start of classes, I joined the ranks of lecturers carrying their shoes in their hands before negotiating the flooded ground and then putting them on again once we reached dry ground.

We got to know more Christian students as we continued to attend the Baptist church. Most were from different faculties – engineering, computer science and nursing. These young believers started attending our Thursday evening cell group too. Very few of these students were from Christian homes, and the majority had no Christian fellowship other than at church and at the cell group.

It was at about that time that a sweet-faced young woman, Aporn Thiengkunakrit, began to feature in our lives. She was not a student, but a salesperson for Myrexware. Initially puzzled by the unfamiliar name, we soon found out that this was another name for Pyrex. Aporn was the only Christian in her family. Although she had no support or fellowship from her parents or other family members in her newly found faith, she was staunch in her belief. Her spiritual life extended to her work and the contacts made through her work. We were greatly encouraged when we heard of a meeting of international heads of Myrex, held in Aporn's home. The president of the company had come from Mexico and others at the meeting had come from different countries. Aporn was not overawed.

As they sat in her sitting room, she made a request. 'I should like to open in prayer,' she said in her soft voice.

'But this is a business meeting, not a religious one!' objected the president.

'I know that this is a business meeting,' replied Aporn,

'but this is my house, and my house belongs to God.' No further objections were raised as Aporn prayed, asking the Lord to be present at their meeting.

Aporn is still an active member of the church, especially in the work among the university students and other young people. She also has a pleasant soprano voice that she uses with dedication and sincerity in singing spiritual songs and solos whenever she is asked. When we were there, Aporn was a little older than most of the students, acting as an older sister, always available to advise and care for them in their problems. Of course, all those students graduated some years ago and many left to work in Bangkok and elsewhere, but Aporn still keeps in touch with them, ready to advise or help. She calls them her 'lambs', feeling the same love and responsibility for them as a shepherd would.

In our flat's tiny kitchen I could cook only simple, easy meals. Eddie accepted whatever I put before him (just as he has done all our married life). Sometimes in the evenings, when I was very tired after a day in the hospital, we would go out to one of the street vendors to buy a plate of noodles. One street in particular was known for its delicious fried noodles. Rickety tables and flimsy stools were arranged to one side of the quiet street ready for customers, while one could see inside the open-fronted kitchen as these noodles were prepared in a wok over a high gas flame. Of course there were restaurants and coffee shops in abundance in Hat Yai, but it cost more to eat in one of these.

Occasionally we would invite a group of students from the cell group to go out for a meal. We would choose a large round table that could accommodate the group of eight or ten, and then each one would be given the opportunity to choose a dish to make up the meal. These dishes were placed in the centre of the table on a rotating 'lazy Susan' so that we could each take our pick in turn. Meanwhile, a large plate of fragrant, steaming rice was put before each person, and a variety of sauces were grouped here and there. Each place was set with a spoon and a fork. We found we were expected to eat with the spoon and use the fork simply to help fill the spoon. A fork was never to be put in the mouth, and a knife was never used at all. To our initial horror, we found that it was perfectly acceptable to serve yourself from a dish with your own spoon that had already been in your mouth. We soon learned to order serving spoons at the same time as we ordered the food! When the bill arrived after the meal, all the students craned their necks in order to see the amount charged – and, without fail, told Eddie that he had been grossly overcharged and that they knew of a cheaper place to eat.

Once in a while we would invite a Thai doctor and his wife to a meal in our flat. The first time, I prepared a special meal and had everything ready on time, only to find that they simply failed to turn up. The second time we made such an arrangement, we reminded the doctor nearer the day, but the same thing happened – Eddie and I were in our best clothes, the table was set and the food was in the oven, but no guests appeared. At last, after consulting with some of our student friends, we realised that this was a cultural thing. No Thai likes to hurt anyone who invites him out by refusing the invitation, so he will always accept, whether or not he really intends to arrive. This explanation helped us to understand the Thai, but it did not help me in organising and cooking meals. Eventually we found a solution: whenever we gave an invitation that was accepted, we always then asked the guest-to-be, 'Are you accepting our invitation *bap Thai rhy bap farang* – the Thai way or the foreigners' way?'

After some time we transferred from the Faculty of Medicine to the Faculty of Dentistry. Dr Krassenai, the Vice Dean of that faculty, was very keen for all dental students to be taught the basics of both surgery and anaesthetics, because the Thai government had the policy of providing one doctor and one dentist in every rural hospital. Krassenai felt strongly that a dentist who understood surgery and knew how to give basic anaesthesia would be a tremendous asset to the lonely doctors, scattered through these regions.

While we had been working in the Faculty of Medicine our salaries had been meagre. The reason for this was that all the other doctors on the staff had private clinics in the afternoons and evenings and these were very lucrative. We felt that, although it was not easy to survive on the low salary, because we had come as missionaries who had been called to work in the university, we should work only there and not engage in private clinics simply to earn more money. However, when we started working in the Dental Faculty, we found that our salaries were double what we had been getting and were now equivalent to 500 US dollars a month. We were grateful for the increase because of all the additional financial demands that seemed to be part of a lecturer's life. Each month a certain amount was deducted automatically from our salaries to cover the cost of coffee available in the hospital (which one might or might not consume). We were expected to contribute towards gifts for colleagues' birthdays, and there were other obligations too. Each lecturer had the responsibility of transporting a group of students from one town to another for training.

Then a complication arose. Our income was now enough to make us liable for income tax. Eddie picked up forms from the Dean's office, filled them in and took them to the tax office in Songkhla. Some time later he received a message summoning him back to the tax office. The head clerk looked at him and shook his head. 'This is quite wrong!' he said. 'You *can't* pay so much tax. No one else from the university pays that much.' And he corrected the forms to his own satisfaction before handing them back to Eddie.

Once the forms had been filled in again, Eddie took them back to Songkhla and paid the required amount, receiving his receipt from the head clerk. 'I usually get a bottle of whisky,' said the clerk.

'I don't do that,' Eddie responded.

The clerk looked put out for a moment. Then he leaned forward. 'Do you see this lump in front of my left ear?' he asked. Eddie nodded. 'It's been taken out twice already,' the clerk went on, 'but it's come back again. Will you cut it out for me?'

Eddie agreed and later operated on the clerk, who was well satisfied with this 'reward' for his services.

It was difficult for Christian students at the university. They were a very tiny minority among the crowd of Buddhist lecturers and students. No concessions were made for those students who wished to attend church on Sundays, so their attendance at Sunday morning worship services was a bit erratic, through no fault of their own. The first year that we were on the staff, examinations happened to be scheduled on Christmas Day. We wondered what else we could do to nurture and teach these young Christians, besides holding the cell group meetings. The first thing Eddie did was to teach them to sing as a choir. They enjoyed this hugely, as did the congregation of the church when the choir had the opportunity to sing during worship services. To this day these students, now graduates, still speak of the hymn they loved to sing most, *'nyng kow nyng'* (Number 191 – 'When peace like a river').

But we felt that taking the choir was not enough. Eddie and I thought back to our own student days, especially about the camps that had been organised by the Student Christian Association. We remembered how the very atmosphere of being at camp, away from all stresses and demands on our time, had been conducive to opening up to the gospel and to more mature teaching of the Christian life. When an opportunity presented itself through a notice of the sale of a mini-van, together with a most generous monetary gift towards our work, Eddie took the opportunity without delay and bought the mini-van for 2,000 baht (approximately 100 US dollars). It had holes in the floorboards through which we could see the road surface. The students laughed and said, 'We have natural air conditioning!' We called the van 'Vera', after the lady who had donated the money. From that time we were able to take a vanload of students away for a day, or sometimes a weekend, camping overnight at various leisure locations in South Thailand. Sometimes Dr Krassenai joined us. These short camps were a great success. At one campsite we found that the sleeping accommodation consisted of one large room for the whole group – men and women, married or single – and our initial reaction was negative. But soon, in spite of our conservative Western background, we accepted this practice and it worked well, with women and men dressing separately without any embarrassment.

After being in the Dental Faculty for some months I found that I was expected to write a short book on basic anaesthesia for the dental students. Dr Krassenai said he would translate it into Thai. This added to my already full workload and I often had to take work home with me. One evening, quite late, I was writing away at our dining table when I suddenly became aware that I was stone deaf and I could not even hear through my one good ear. I stopped working straight away and went to bed.

In the morning my hearing in that ear had recovered. Nonetheless, I remembered how the Ménière's disease had started years before, also with episodes of sudden, complete deafness, and I wondered if my only good ear was also going to become totally deaf. On Eddie's advice, I told Dr Krassenai about it. I said that, regrettably, I would not be able to stay on the university staff any longer. He understood and let me resign. Eddie and I then informed our OMF Superintendent, who passed on the information to the Director for Thailand. In due course, OMF invited us to go and work at the OMF hospital in Saiburi, also in South Thailand. My problem had been understood, as I was told I would not be expected to give anaesthetics or do any medical work, as the stress involved might cause a recurrence of the deafness in my good ear. Eddie was to replace Dr John Garland as Medical Superintendent of Saiburi Hospital, as Dr Garland and his wife were leaving Thailand to return to the UK. Sooner than I could have thought possible, we were on our way to the village of Saiburi, in the coastal region off the Gulf of Thailand.

16

Independent Years

And my God shall supply all your need.
(Philippians 4:19)

Eddie and I arrived at the coastal town of Saiburi to find it was set in beautiful surroundings. Gleaming white sandy beaches contrasted with the unbelievably blue-green water broken by white-edged wavelets, and stately palms with curving trunks formed a tropical background. A missionary from the hospital met us at the railway station, welcomed us warmly and gave us a meal at a small restaurant nearby before accompanying us in a taxi to the hospital compound. We were shown around the hospital and introduced to the staff, both missionary and Thai. Our new home was a comfortable, spacious house of teak on high stilts, set in an informal garden of shrubs of various kinds. Across from the house, over a river, we could see the white dots of ducks on a Thai duck-farmer's property. We soon settled in and Eddie started his work as Medical Superintendent, while I unpacked and sorted out our belongings. I appreciated the fact that it was generally understood that

I could not give anaesthetics or do medical work at this time.

Our new home had shutters for its windows, but needed half-length curtains so we could have privacy and still be able to feel the cool breeze coming from the sea. One afternoon we went into the village to choose and buy some cotton material so that I could make the curtains. A few days after we had acquired the material, there was a knock at our front door. There stood the OMF Superintendent responsible for South Thailand. He took our breath away with his surprise announcement that OMF wanted us back in Manorom rather than in Saiburi, and that both Eddie and I were to work full time at the hospital. We were staggered by this sudden change of direction, as we had been in Saiburi only a few weeks. The Superintendent went on to say that, out of consideration for my ear condition, I could have a short holiday before starting work, but after the holiday I would have to start work as an anaesthetist again. Eddie expostulated on my behalf, reminding him that OMF's South Thailand Field Council had given me permission *not* to do medical work because of the danger of me becoming totally deaf in both ears. The Superintendent suggested that we take a weekend away from the hospital so that we 'could pray about it'.

And so we took the weekend away from Saiburi Hospital and stayed in a reasonably priced hotel in Hat Yai, where we used the time to be quiet, praying individually about this development. At the end of the weekend I said to Eddie, 'Well, after praying a lot about it, I have peace about going back to Manorom. Even if it should mean that I become 100 per cent deaf in both ears, I am willing for that if it is the Lord's will.'

He replied, 'And as for me, after all these hours of prayer, I am utterly convinced that, as your husband, I must look after you and I cannot allow you to go to Manorom to work in the hospital at this time.'

On our return to Saiburi Eddie told the Director of our decision not to go to Manorom. 'But it is the considered intention of OMF to close down Saiburi Hospital and to run it simply as a leprosy clinic,' he said. 'You can't stay on here!' But Eddie remained adamant that I should not work full time. He said we could certainly go to Manorom, but that only he would work in the hospital, while I could do other, less stressful work than that of giving anaesthetics.

Not long after that interview, we were given an opportunity to see the Field Director for the whole of Thailand. When he remonstrated with us for being unwilling to obey our leaders' directive, I asked him, 'If I were to go to Manorom and work there, and if I were then to become completely deaf in both ears, would you be willing to take that responsibility?'

And he stunned me by replying, 'Yes!' My first reaction of disbelief at his reply was lessened by the realisation that he was not a doctor with medical training.

We knew that we could not obey our OMF leaders because of health reasons. We also firmly believed that members of a mission should always be obedient to their leaders. For that reason, the only honourable thing for us to do was to resign from OMF. We did not want to resign. But we also did not feel it was right to stay on if we could not follow instructions from the Mission's leaders. It was therefore with very deep regret that we handed in our resignation. We remembered the way God had called us into the

OMF and how certain we had been of His call, how willingly we had left our work, home and family to work in Thailand with OMF.

We were now in a kind of limbo. We were far from home, without any income and without definite direction for our lives. We packed up again and left the pleasant home in Saiburi that we had enjoyed for such a brief time, but where were we to go from there? And what were we to do? In a kind of reflex action we returned to the one other place we knew best in South Thailand – Hat Yai. There, as we spoke to Revd Jack Mahaffey, the minister of the Baptist church we had attended while working at the university, we found that he had a most opportune and immediate solution to our problem. Jack offered us use, rent free, of the new building in the church grounds that was meant to house a Thai pastor once he himself had returned to America. The church council supported his idea. This meant that while we stayed there we would be available to assist with the church work, especially among the students and youth in the congregation. We knew that the Thai love to sing, especially in harmony, and Eddie soon organised a student choir. This choir sang in the church from time to time and was used by God as a means of blessing the whole congregation.

We soon settled into our new accommodation. Our only expense was that of buying food, so the small amount of money we had in the bank was sufficient for some months. We had not told anyone at all – either in Thailand or at home in South Africa – that we now had no money coming in. By mutual consent we simply committed it to the Lord in prayer and trusted Him to look after us in these new circumstances. Inevitably, the day came when our bank account was almost empty. Suddenly, a thought came into my mind. When she died, my mother had left me a ring with a large solitaire diamond. The diamond was so large that I knew I would never wear the ring, but we could not afford to pay bank charges to keep it in safe deposit, so I had brought it with us to Thailand wrapped in a tissue and inside a small plastic bank bag.

'What about Mom's ring?' I asked Eddie excitedly. 'We can sell that. I'm sure we'll get enough money for it to live on for quite some time!'

'All right, if you're willing to sell it,' answered Eddie, relief evident in his voice. 'We can go to Bangkok to the Chinese quarter. There are a great many jewellery shops in Chinatown and I'm sure you'll sell it easily there.'

We boarded the train at Hat Yai station and travelled overnight to Bangkok. First of all we contacted Apithan, who had graduated by then and was working in a hospital in the city. He gave us good advice and the names and addresses of shops that were likely to want to buy the dia-mond ring. After many bus trips and miles of walking the streets of Chinatown, we eventually found the right shop. The owner examined the stone meticulously and made us an offer: 360,000 baht![1] Our minds boggled at the thought of how long that amount of money would last us. The owner of the shop asked us if we would prefer cash or a cheque, and immediately we both replied, 'Cash, please.' We were unsure if we could trust a cheque from this shop. He counted out and gave us a thick wad of notes. After

---

[1] Approximately US$14,000.

counting them himself, Eddie placed the notes inside the plastic shopping bag I had brought with me for that purpose. It was surely more appropriate for carrying groceries than money – but that was the reason why I had brought the bag with me. There we were, in casual cotton clothes, sandals on our bare feet, about to catch a bus back to the central district of Bangkok. I had said to Eddie that if we looked as if we were poor, and I was carrying a plastic bag, no would-be thief would entertain the idea that we could have with us such a large amount of money. And so it proved. We returned to the business district of Bangkok and deposited the princely sum in a bank. For the next few years we would be able to manage.

While we were living in Hat Yai, a worker with the Christian organisation World Vision approached Eddie on their behalf. They asked him to work for them by conducting medical clinics for prisoners in the large jail serving the nearby coastal towns of Songkhla and Nakorn Sri Thammarat. In return, Eddie would be paid a monthly sum of money. Eddie was glad to have received the invitation, but unfortunately the monthly income they were offering would not be sufficient to pay the rent of a house in Songkhla as well as our food and other basic expenses. Once more we told nobody about our dilemma, but prayed earnestly, waiting on the Lord to reveal His will to us. We had no idea how the Lord would supply our need, and when He did so it came like a bolt from the blue.

One morning the postman delivered an airmail letter from South Africa to us. We looked eagerly at the return address. It had been sent from Revd Kobus Thom, the chairman of the missions arm of the NG Kerk (Dutch Reformed

Church). In the envelope was the answer to our prayers – a gift from the church of 72,000 baht,[2] which was exactly the amount we would need to rent a house in Songkhla for two years. As Kobus wrote, this gift was to provide *'n kasteel vir Dorothy* (a castle for Dorothy). The Lord's timing was perfect. We thanked Him from the bottom of our hearts.

We found a suitable house in Songkhla. It was roomy and comfortable, with air conditioning in the lounge and bedrooms. There was a small front garden with shrubs and a large grassy area behind the house with an old, gnarled tamarind tree. It even had an extra room for a house-help, or maid. Some time after we had moved in we were asked if we could give a job as house-help to a young Thai woman with the nickname *Mow*.[3] We went to fetch her and found her a pleasant, smiling, plump girl of about 17, who had never worked before. When we showed her the room in which she was to sleep her face fell and she begged us to let her sleep on the floor in the dining room. She would remove her bedding from the floor early each morning. It turned out that she was absolutely terrified of evil spirits that might attack her at night if she slept in her own room. We had found this profound fear of evil spirits common to many of our Thai Buddhist patients in Central Thailand, with some female patients too frightened to unbutton their blouses so that we could listen to their chests with a stethoscope. Women in that rural area even kept on their outer sarong-like garment when they bathed in the river, for fear that evil spirits should see their bodies.

---

[2] $2,700.

[3] Cat.

Mow soon settled in, keeping house for us while we went to hold clinics in the prison. She walked to market early each morning to buy fresh produce and cooked tasty Thai meals. As she became used to working for two *farang* who were away from the house for hours at a time, her routine gradually became more and more relaxed. Eventually she would put lunch on the table as soon as she had cleared away the breakfast dishes, even though it was still only 9 o'clock in the morning. For the rest of the day, whether we were in the house or not, she sat on the plastic-covered couch in the lounge and watched Thai television. No amount of gentle remonstrating with her helped. When we could not face eating yet another lunch of cold curry, Eddie drove her back to her home and parents. On the way she implored us to say nothing to her parents about why we did not want her to work for us any longer – and so, of course, we said nothing about it. In any case, by that time I had become used to our new surroundings and was able to cope on my own.

The prisons in which we held our clinics were huge and covered a large area of ground – one prison for men and a separate, smaller prison for women. These two compounds were some distance from each other. There were practically no amenities at all for the prisoners. Dormitories were huge, like hangars, with concrete floors. The prisoners slept on the concrete like rows of sardines, without even reed mats to soften the surface a little. The dormitory doors were locked at 4 o'clock each afternoon, with the prisoners all inside together, and were opened again only at 6 o'clock the next morning. The grounds were well kept (by the prisoners themselves), but we saw no benches along the concrete paths. A warder later told us that the prisoners were there to be punished – they did not deserve a place to sit down – and that they should have thought before they committed their crimes. I was allowed free entrance to the female prison for my clinics, but if for any reason I had to go into the male prison I was not allowed in unescorted. The risk of being taken hostage was ever present. During the few times I was in the male prison, accompanied by a prison official, his eyes were alert and roving as he continually looked for danger.

The women prisoners were mainly drug addicts or drug pushers. I saw few women at my clinics who were genuinely ill. Most of the women who lined up waiting to be seen wanted to con the doctor (me) into prescribing drugs that they could hoard, dry out under the burning, tropical sun and then grind into a powder. They would then either sniff up the powder into their nostrils or else dissolve it in water and then inject it into their veins to get a high. They were so desperate for drugs that they even used aspirin or paracetamol tablets for this purpose. I soon learned to prescribe only a few tablets at a time, to reduce the possibility of hoarding. A favourite complaint was that they could not sleep. Either they wanted a note from the doctor to say they must be given a reed mat because their backs hurt from lying on the concrete floor, or they wanted me to prescribe a sleeping tablet for them. I refused to prescribe sleeping tablets because of the danger of addiction, but sometimes I did prescribe a mild tranquilliser. I stopped doing even this when I found out that these tablets were not being used as prescribed, but were being sniffed or injected. These women were hardened, and opportunities to talk to them about Christ were few and far between.

The men's prison was not only much larger than the women's, it was much more crowded as well. In contrast to my clinics at the women's prison, Eddie found that most of the prisoners who attended his clinics were genuinely ill. The fact that many of them were multiple murderers was of little importance. When he first arrived the warders showed him to a small, airless, austerely furnished room in which he was to conduct his clinics. It was very hot and stuffy, and did not even have a fan. Eddie told the head warder that this room was most unsuitable and persuaded him to let him hold his clinics in the open air of the veranda adjacent to the small room originally allocated for the clinic. This was a great improvement.

One day a young man named Prasert attended the clinic. He complained of shortness of breath, exacerbated by the fairly strenuous PT sessions that were compulsory for the male prisoners. On examining his chest, Eddie found that he had a large pleural effusion[4] on the right side. The contents of his chest cavity were pushed over to the left side by the large amount of fluid present. His heart, too, was pushed over at right angles to the normal position, with the strong apex beat of the heart easily discernible in his left armpit instead of the middle of the left side of his chest. This patient needed urgent admission to a hospital for immediate surgery to drain off the fluid and to relieve the pressure inside his chest. When Eddie reported this to the head warder and asked him to arrange immediate admission to hospital, the head warder declined to do so.

'If we let a patient be admitted to hospital, he will

---

[4] Fluid within the chest cavity.

undoubtedly escape,' he said. 'This has happened before. If this patient needs something to be done, doctor, you must do it yourself, right here in the prison grounds.' So Eddie found himself in the unfamiliar position of operating in the bright, warm sunlight of the prison yard, while he inserted a drainage catheter into Prasert's chest cavity. He was concerned about the possibility of sepsis at the site of his incision into the chest wall because the procedure had not been done in a sterile hospital environment, so he persuaded prison officials to let Prasert sleep in the small room originally intended for the clinic, with a guard to watch over him. In order to minimise the very real risk of sepsis Eddie removed the drainage catheter earlier than he would normally have done. This meant that some fluid still remained in the chest cavity, but this would be absorbed gradually by the body's own mechanisms. It also meant that when Eddie saw Prasert on one of his post-operative checks, he was not in the least surprised when Prasert told him that whenever he ran, he felt a 'splashing' inside his chest!

Because Eddie saw Prasert more often than the other patients, he had more opportunity to speak to him about faith in Christ Jesus as his personal Saviour. The young man listened attentively, hanging on every word. One day he told Eddie that he had prayed to Christ to forgive his sins and to become his Saviour. Smiling broadly, he said, 'My heart is in the right place since you operated on me – and my spiritual heart is now also in the right place!'

Neither male nor female prisoners had any access to dental treatment. Eddie was shocked to see the poor condition of the teeth of many male prisoners. He asked the head warder about the possibility of arranging for a dentist to make regular visits to the prison, but the head warder laughed and said again that these prisoners were in the jail for punishment and they should have thought before they committed their crimes. Then Eddie asked a dentist friend to teach him how to give local anaesthetic injections that would eliminate the pain of dental extractions. Soon he was adept at performing a sensory block of one side of the jaw. He collected 20 men with the worst dental decay and lined them up. Starting at one end of the row, he injected their jaws in turn. By the time he had finished injecting the tenth man the first one's jaw was completely numb and Eddie could start with the necessary extractions. This organised approach saved him from having to wait each time for individual injections to work before he set to work to pull the decayed teeth. Occasionally Eddie would come to the women's prison and perform dental extractions there too. I shall never forget their broad, gap-toothed smiles after they realised that their toothache was gone for ever.

One Friday morning Eddie woke before dawn with the urgent conviction that he should travel north to Manorom Christian Hospital that same day. He knew that we were expected at the prison at 8 o'clock that morning and did not know how to reconcile this urge to go to Manorom with our commitment to the usual prison work. Mulling it over, he fell into a fitful sleep again until 7 o'clock, when he shared his inner conviction with me. We discussed this, but did not know what to do about it. Manorom is far from Songkhla (about 1,200 kilometres), and to go there would take Eddie the whole day. It was not possible to telephone Manorom to find out if there was a special need, as the hospital had no telephone at that time. We thought of sending a telegram, but discarded the idea immediately as a telegram might not reach Manorom until after the weekend. Eddie decided to have his regular morning time of Bible reading and prayer. He thought that perhaps during his reading he might receive guidance. But he received no such guidance. Instead, his conviction grew stronger. Finally he decided that we should go to the prison at 8 o'clock as arranged. We should work in our clinics until 11 o'clock. If his strange conviction persisted, he would cut his clinic short, fetch me and go home to make inquiries as to how best he could get to Manorom. This we did, and by 11 o'clock his inner urge was stronger than ever. We left the prison, not knowing exactly what was to happen next. What actually did happen is a story in itself.

17

Mrs Uthai

Then He said to the woman, 'Your faith has saved
you.'

(Luke 7:50)

I *wonder – what will she be like?* As Eddie climbed the
stairs to the women's surgical ward, his thoughts were
on the patient he had operated on the night before.
When he had been called to theatre to help in a difficult
emergency operation, the patient had already been anaesthetised and her body covered by sterile drapes except for
the abdomen. The young doctor who had been unable to
complete the operation himself told Eddie that all he knew
about the patient was that she was Mrs Uthai, aged 68, from
Manorom village, and she was critically ill.

Eddie reached the single-bedded ward and opened the
door. A faint smell of anaesthetic still hung in the air.
Instead of the miserable, weak patient he was expecting to
see after the long and complicated surgery she had under-
gone just ten hours earlier, he saw a small, elderly lady sitting up in bed with her bright, intelligent eyes fixed on his
own. An oxygen cylinder was standing alongside her bed.

'Good morning, Mrs Uthai,' he began in Thai. 'You won't

know who I am. I am the surgeon who operated on you last night. My name is Dr Rose. How do you feel this morning?'

'Very much better than yesterday, thank you, doctor,' she replied. Her voice was surprisingly strong and clear.

'You know, Mrs Uthai, God must love you very much!'

She gazed at him with a quizzical expression (she was, of course, a Buddhist), and he went on: 'You see, yesterday God compelled me to leave my work in South Thailand – something I would never normally do – and to come to Manorom. When I arrived, I was just in time to operate on you. Would you like to hear all about it?'

Mrs Uthai nodded. And then Eddie told her all that had happened to him the day before, from the very beginning. . .

He had been in his bedroom in Songkhla, over 1,000 kilometres away. In the very early morning he had suddenly come awake. By the small suggestion of light that precedes the dawn he could make out the shapes of furniture in the room. Cocks were crowing in the distance. Through the open windows a slight breeze brought him the scent of flowers in the garden. He wondered what had woken him and realised it was a strong inner conviction that he must go to Manorom Hospital that very day. He knew he was not free to travel that day, however, because he had a clinic to hold at Songkhla prison. He started the clinic, but, still feeling that conviction – stronger than ever – he left early. He just *had* to get to Manorom.

The trains to Bangkok were fully booked for the next five days, so his only option was to fly there on the scheduled flight from South Thailand at 12.15. On inquiring at the domestic airways office, he found there was one vacant seat left and he hastily booked it. The time was then 11.20 a.m.

He could buy the ticket at the airport in Hat Yai, but first he needed cash to pay for it. He drove quickly to the bank and found the usual Friday morning crush of people standing waiting. He joined one of the four queues that snaked inside the bank, almost to the door. His heart sank at the prospect of a long delay. But God was with him, and as he stood, almost quivering with impatience, an amazing thing happened. A teller behind the counter, ignoring the other clients in the queue, called out to him, 'Dr Rose, what can I do for you?'

'I need 4,000 baht!' said Eddie, lifting up his savings book.

'Here is the money,' said the teller, taking the notes out of the drawer in front of him and holding them up.

'What about my savings book?' asked Eddie, still holding it up.

'Don't worry about that now – just come and sign this form to say you've received the money. We can fill in the book later.'

The teller had no idea that Eddie was in a great hurry. Yet Eddie's time in the bank had been less than a minute, in spite of it having been a busy Friday morning. He rushed out and scrambled back into the car, where I was waiting, and said to me, 'Well, I'm certainly convinced now that the Lord really does want me to go to Manorom today!'

By the time he had driven home to toss a few necessities into an overnight bag it was already 11.40. We knew that the plane was due to take off from Hat Yai in 35 minutes, and that Hat Yai airport was 55 kilometres away. Passengers were required to check in 20 minutes before departure. Eddie lost no time in driving off, as fast as he could. Unfortunately he was delayed by an unexpected number of cars and motorcycles on the road, so we arrived at 12.05, ten minutes after the deadline. Bowing his head and with his hands together in the Thai manner to show respect, Eddie apologised profusely for his lateness. 'Never mind,' the clerk reassured him. 'The plane has been delayed by a technical fault, and you are still in time!' This was another persuasive indication that God wanted him in Manorom that very day. The plane arrived at Bangkok at 1.30 p.m. From the airport Eddie took a taxi to Bangkok's northern bus station and caught the first tour bus to Manorom. By the time the bus stopped to let him off at the entrance of the lane that leads to Manorom Christian Hospital, it was already dusk. He set off up the lane.

As he walked through the hospital gate he met a fellow missionary coming towards him. 'Hello, Ed, this is a surprise! What brings you to Manorom?'

'I don't know quite why I'm here,' replied Eddie truthfully.

'Well,' said the fellow missionary, 'you'd better go on up to the guest house and find yourself a room for the night.'

Eddie did as his friend suggested. He was on the way to his room when the telephone on the wall outside rang shrilly. Eddie answered. It was Dr Peter Farrington, the hospital's Medical Director, who wanted to speak to him. *News certainly travels fast here,* Eddie thought. *I've only just arrived!*

'I heard that you were here in Manorom,' said Peter. 'I hope you haven't made a mistake in the date of our meeting next month!'

'No,' replied Eddie, and he explained about the strong inner conviction he had felt to come to the hospital that day.

No sooner had Eddie replaced the handset than it started ringing once more. The call was again for him. An urgent voice spoke rapidly in his ear. 'Ed, I've just heard that you're here, and I need you in theatre right away! Can you come over and help me? I've just started an emergency operation and everything is distorted and I don't know what to do!'

Eddie dumped his bag in his room and ran over to the operating suite, put on surgical tunic, trousers and a mask, scrubbed his hands and was gowned. The Swiss doctor made way for Eddie and crossed over to the assistant's position. With Eddie's experience in surgery, in spite of the sepsis and adhesions that distorted the anatomy he was able to ascertain that the patient had had a ruptured appendix for some weeks, resulting in multiple abscesses. The appendix was gangrenous. Carefully and painstakingly he worked, dealt successfully with the matted, inflamed bowel and drained the abscesses. Finally the last sutures were inserted and the patient was taken back to the ward.

The whole time Eddie spoke, Mrs Uthai's eyes remained on his face, as he told her of the events leading up to his arrival in Manorom and the crucial part he believed God had played in bringing him in time for her life-saving operation.

'You see now, Mrs Uthai, why I said that God must love you very, very much. He had to shake me out of my routine and out of my rigid, conservative attitude until I was willing to do things in an unorthodox way, even though I did not yet know what He wanted me to do!' he ended.

She was silent, rapt with attention.

'Do you want to hear more about this God who loves you so much?'

Mrs Uthai nodded emphatically.

And so Eddie began at the very beginning, telling her the

story of creation and then of God's plan of salvation for sinful men by sending His only Son, Jesus Christ, to die on the cross in their place. Never once did her gaze falter. From time to time she nodded in wonder and approval. When he had finished, he asked her if she wanted to put her trust in this great God and to believe in Jesus Christ as her Saviour. She agreed emphatically. Without hesitation she accepted the Lord and when Eddie prayed, she repeated the words of Eddie's prayer.

Eddie was thrilled at Mrs Uthai's response. As he left her ward to go back to the guest house to collect his overnight bag, his heart was singing. But then questions came into his mind, draining some of his enthusiasm. *What if she really didn't understand all I said? My Thai isn't all that wonderful. Could a person who has been a Buddhist for many years really have accepted Christ just like that?*

He decided that before he left to catch his bus he would telephone *Acharn* Somsak, the Thai pastor of Manorom Church, and ask him to see Mrs Uthai. *Acharn* Somsak readily agreed to see her later that morning. With a lighter heart once more, Eddie left the hospital, leaving the Manorom doctors in charge of Mrs Uthai's post-operative care. The prospect of the long journey home – a three-hour bus journey to Bangkok and an overnight train trip – did not seem arduous to him at all.

One day, three weeks after his return to Songkhla, Eddie received three letters from Manorom, all saying virtually the same thing. Peter Farrington wrote,

Ed, when you operated on her, you didn't know who Mrs Uthai was, and how important and influential she is in Manorom village. She's always been an exceptionally staunch Buddhist and whenever she heard of someone in the village who wanted to become a Christian, she went to see them and argued so persuasively that many prospective converts reverted to Buddhism. She even took some of these people by the hand, to lead them back to the Buddhist temple! At first we here found it impossible to believe that she had become converted to Christianity herself, because of her past history over the last 25 years, but she has changed radically, and we are now satisfied that she has really turned from Buddhism to Christ!

When he had finished reading the letter, Eddie said to me, 'If ever I should have a similar urge or conviction again, however strange it might be, I'll be sure to obey it straight away next time!'

Mrs Uthai lived on in Manorom for another eleven or twelve years, her love for the Lord undiminished in spite of determined efforts by several Buddhist friends. When Mrs Uthai's husband died suddenly and unexpectedly, her friends warned her that this was punishment for leaving Buddhism, but Mrs Uthai did not budge. Later, her 46-year-old son died also, and her friends renewed their clamour for her to return to Buddhism before even more tragedy could strike. The spirits were displeased with her, they said. Mrs Uthai remained faithful to her Lord. She initiated a weekly cell group in her home. This became not only a means of fellowship and discipleship for young Christians, but also an outreach to those who would not attend Manorom Church. When other Thai believers visited her from time to time she encouraged them all in their walk with the Lord. And when the time came for her to die, there was joy even in the sorrow of her passing, as she had gone to eternal life with her Lord.

18

Manorom and Malawi

Make this fellow return, that he may go back to
the place which you have appointed for him.

(1 Samuel 29:4)

While we were living in Songkhla, Dr Peter Farrington got in touch with Eddie to ask him to go up to Manorom to see him the following month. When the day came, Eddie went up to Manorom by train and bus, wondering all the time why Peter wanted to see him.

In Peter's office at last, they greeted each other warmly. Then Peter came straight to the point of the interview. 'Ed, I want you here at Manorom,' he began. 'We need another surgeon badly. We have only one surgeon here. Since John Townsend left, Neil Thompson has had to do all emergency calls as well as his regular work.'

'But –' began Eddie.

'Yes, I know I can't take you back as OMF missionaries,' Peter interposed. 'I know you and Dorothy resigned from the Mission. But I also know that you resigned only because you felt you couldn't comply with OMF's directive that you should both work full time. I've had an idea! I can't take you back as OMF missionaries, but I'm allowed to employ Thai doctors, paying them a salary. If you're willing to come, I will employ you on the same terms as I would a Thai doctor, giving you a house in the hospital compound, rent free.'

'I'm sure Dorothy will gladly agree with me that we should take up your offer,' said Eddie. 'I'll tell her as soon as I get back to Songkhla.'

And that was how we came back to Manorom, where the Lord had called us originally. It was good to be back, even if I was no longer able to work in the hospital itself. Peter was as good as his word and allotted us a house in the hospital compound. This house was on stilts, Thai style, and made of wood. There were high wooden steps to the front and back of the house, with posts on each side. It had many windows that we kept open at all times so they could catch the slightest breeze. This meant that it *felt* cooler even on the hottest days, when the inside temperature was 104°F. OMF had also allotted us a pleasant woman to act as house-help. Kimbua was rather older than the usual domestic worker in staff homes, but we were glad of this as she had much more experience in cooking and cleaning and it was never necessary to correct her in the acceptable tactful way.

To get to our house from the hospital it was easiest and most direct to approach it from the back. The drawback of doing that, however, was that the base of the back steps was a favourite haunt of poisonous snakes and we had to be on constant lookout for these. In daylight this was easy, but when Eddie was called out at night he went out and returned with some trepidation.

These snakes became much more of a menace when we acquired a cat we called Candy. The snakes fascinated him. He would bring a snake or two into the house to show us how clever he was, lying on the floor near them. In the house we walked about barefoot, so we had to learn to step right over these reptiles. At night Candy's favourite dumping place for the snakes was on the floor in the passage just outside our bedroom door, so we would see them in the morning when we got up. The trouble was that the bathroom was opposite our bedroom on the other side of the passage and each time either of us needed to pay a visit to the bathroom at night we ran the very real risk of stepping on one of these adders. How Candy avoided getting bitten was a mystery that we never solved.

Eddie welcomed the opportunity to use his specialist skills again and was kept really busy with routine surgical work in the day and with surgical emergencies at night. Because of the shortage of experienced surgeons at Manorom, he was sometimes on call for weeks at a time. I, however, took on less demanding jobs, as I was excused from hospital work for the sake of my health. I took on the job of Medical Advisor to the Central Thailand field. This meant that I would undertake regular medical examinations of OMF missionaries stationed in Central Thailand, treat any illnesses and give general medical advice where indicated. After each examination I was required to send in a report to OMF Headquarters in Singapore, to the doctor in charge over all fields. Once it became known that there was a doctor specifically for this duty, missionaries from other mission organisations also started to come for regular check-ups. This meant that I got to know many other

Christian missionaries whom I would not otherwise have met.

These examinations did not take up all my time by any means, so I volunteered for the unpopular job of selling stamps to missionaries who, for one reason or another, could not get to Manorom post office. For an hour in the mornings, two days a week, I used to sit at a table in the upstairs library-cum-prayer room, with books of stamps all around me. Missionaries would drift in from time to time with their requests. Selling stamps was not arduous, but counting up and reconciling my account book was much more work. Some missionaries would take their stamps and leave without remembering to pay – and that meant I would have to trace them and remind them. Others would pay and forget to take their change. The accounting often took me much longer than the selling and sometimes I nearly missed my lunch. Some nights I even dreamed about the figures I could not get to balance.

Another outlet for me was to take a basic Bible study with Kimbua, our house-help, and a friend of hers called Phikun, who worked in the kitchen of the guest house. We three would sit around the dining table in our house. I taught them to memorise key Bible verses in Thai (17 years later I can still repeat these verses in Thai, having gone over them so often). Kimbua was a professing Christian, while Phikun was a Buddhist. I felt that although my Thai language was adequate, it was not really colloquial enough to convey what I wanted to express so that they would be able to understand and appropriate the meaning of these verses for themselves. I concentrated instead on helping them get to know parts of God's Word, trusting that at a later time these words of life from the Bible would come to their minds and that the Holy Spirit would use them and interpret them. From time to time I also went to help with the larger afternoon groups that Adele Juzi, another missionary, would arrange for all domestic workers in Manorom Hospital.

For a time the administrative office for the hospital was short staffed and I was asked to help there in the earlier part of the mornings. *How can I help?* I thought. *I'm not trained in secretarial work.* Nevertheless, I went there and offered my services. I was to compose and type letters of thanks to all those who had made donations to OMF specifically for Manorom. That did not sound too onerous, but then I found I was meant to type these letters on a computer! I had never used a computer before, and I was petrified. 'It isn't that bad,' comforted the secretary. 'Just sit there. On your left is a small book of hints on WordPerfect. If you really get stuck, just call me to help.' And so, for the first time in my life, I sat nervously before a computer. (It was the start of a closer friendship with that machine, though I did not know it at the time.)

As it happened, I had an unexpected advantage. When we were working in the Faculty of Dentistry at the Prince of Songkhla University, the Vice Dean, Dr Krassenai, had asked me to help him with composing and typing English letters. When I arrived at his office the first afternoon I saw he had an electronic typewriter. It was not too difficult to master the principles of using it. When faced with the computer at Manorom, I found that these principles were identical – and I heaved a great sigh of relief. Each donor was written a different thank-you letter. The Medical Superintendent gave me a list of projects or articles that were benefiting from donations so that I could tell each donor how his or her gift was being used for the hospital.

Eddie never forgot his chief reason for being at Manorom. It was not only to practise surgery for the benefit of patients. In his heart he carried a burning need to tell them of God and of His plan for salvation and freedom from bondage to the spirit world. He was alert to every opportunity that came to him. During this time at Manorom, over a period of little more than a week, he was given the joy of leading four male patients to Christ – Manop, Maniet, Prathip and Mongkon. The stories of two of these men, Prathip and Mongkon, are worth telling.

One afternoon, while he was walking down the hospital corridor, Eddie felt a compulsion to go to Prathip, a man he had operated on two days before, and to tell him of God's plan of salvation. When he came to Prathip's bedside and started speaking of Christ's sacrifice on the cross, Prathip interrupted him, saying eagerly, 'I know why you're here! I had a dream last night and it's been in my thoughts ever since. I dreamt that I was standing in a road at a place where it branched into two. In the wider road I could see my Buddhist friends, beckoning me to join them. The other road was narrow and looked less inviting. In it I saw some people I know to be Christians, who were also beckoning to me to come. I thought and thought about this dream, but I couldn't understand it. Now you've come to tell me of the love of God and of His Son, Jesus Christ. I believe that God sent that dream to me to tell me to decide to follow Him, however difficult it might be!'

Mongkon's story was very different and yet was also incontrovertible evidence of God's power. He had travelled from a remote island in the east part of the Gulf of Thailand in order to visit a relative of his who lived in Chainat Province. While there he had developed symptoms related to his urinary tract and had taken the opportunity to attend the outpatients department of Manorom Hospital. Some days later Eddie performed a prostatectomy on him. The post-operative course went smoothly and in due time Mongkon was ready to be discharged. He was standing next to his bed, with his belongings in a bag at his feet, when Eddie went to see him for the last time, just before he was due in the operating theatre. Eddie cannot remember now how it happened, but their conversation soon turned to spiritual matters and he told Mongkon about salvation. He was startled to find that Mongkon accepted all he said straight away. Unfortunately, Eddie was already late for his surgical list and had to leave for the operating theatre. *Mongkon mustn't go home yet,* he thought. *I must get one of the hospital evangelists to see him immediately, before he leaves the hospital and goes back to his island.*

He raced up to the operating theatre and put out a call for an evangelist to come to theatre immediately. When the evangelists heard the urgent call they thought there must be a dire emergency and one of them rushed to the theatre as quickly as he could. Eddie reassured the evangelist that the emergency was not in the theatre and told him there was a patient in the ward on the point of being discharged who had made a decision to commit himself to the Lord. Eddie wanted the evangelist to see Mongkon before he was sent home, so he could be sure of his decision.

The evangelist did so, and was able to confirm that Mongkon had accepted the Lord. Eddie rejoiced at the news. But then he thought further. He had learnt there were no other Christians on Mongkon's island. Who could disciple this young Christian? Who could teach him more of his new-found faith? For Mongkon to return to loneliness and isolation was not to be considered. Eddie wondered what he could do. Suddenly Apithan came into his mind. He might very well know of other Christians near enough to the island. So he contacted his ex-student, now a doctor with a practice in Bangkok, and it turned out that Apithan knew of a lively church on the mainland, just opposite Mongkon's island. He telephoned the pastor there and confirmed that he and members of his church would visit Mongkon from time to time and have fellowship with him. So Mongkon, although he was the only Christian living on his lonely island, was not left alone but was cared for spiritually from that time onwards.

I remember being told of a young man who lived in a town to the north-west of Manorom, who used to walk back home each evening after work. His usual route led him past a Christian meeting, from which he often heard the sound of singing. One evening he could not resist the temptation of curiosity and entered the hall. A missionary was standing before the people there. When he heard the missionary speak he listened, enthralled. Afterwards he begged to speak to the missionary for a few minutes, and when the way of salvation was explained to him he willingly accepted Christ's death in his place, by faith. Later, he turned to leave. When he reached the door that opened onto the street he came to a sudden halt, his legs frozen. The missionary wondered what was wrong and asked him why he had stopped. His eyes rolling in his head, the young man told the missionary that he could not go home because he could see several evil spirits lying in wait for him just outside the door. The missionary put his arm around him and prayed with him, asking the Lord for deliverance. When the young man opened his eyes again the spirits had vanished and the way was clear for him to go home. This new convert stayed firm in his resolve; not even his family or friends could persuade him to return to Buddhism. He said he had been made free, really free, and could never return to the bondage and fear of evil spirits that was inherent in that religion.

Most conversions to Christianity took place after the preaching of a missionary, coupled with the example of his Christ-centred life. Some took place almost solely through the written word of the Bible. A telling example of this type of conversion is that of a poor man who lived in the province of Uthai in Central Thailand. Let's call him Prichaa. He was uneducated and illiterate, so made his living by selling ice cream. In the tropical heat and humidity he would pedal tirelessly along the streets and lanes of the country town, calling out all the time to attract children, his chief customers. In the afternoons Prichaa would go to the local school gates and park his cycle with its large wooden box. Inside the wooden box were chunks of ice, replenished as necessary, which made sure his ice creams stayed frozen. As streams of children began to emerge through the gates he would call to them, tempting them to buy.

One evening, after his work was over, he was attracted to an open-air meeting where a missionary was preaching. As he stood among the crowd, he listened intently to the missionary's words. Prichaa had never heard anything like it before. He stood, transfixed, as he heard of God's wonderful plan for the salvation of men. He was unable to understand fully all that the missionary said, however, and when the meeting ended he gratefully accepted the leaflet that was being offered to all present. He could not read, of course, but he knew exactly what to do. The next afternoon, as children were leaving the school, he was parked there ready. As children came up to him to buy an ice cream, he first showed them the leaflet that he had been given the night before. He asked each child the meaning of one word, storing it in his memory. It took days before he got the meaning of the tract, which was an extract from John's Gospel, chapter three, but eventually he could understand the message. The seed of God's Word found fruitful soil in his heart and he found salvation in Christ Jesus, the Son of God, who had died for him. He wanted to know more, but neither in his circle of friends nor in his family was there another Christian who could teach him.

Some time later he left his home to find work in another town. He packed his few belongings and took them with him on the bus that would take him to his destination. His heart was heavy as he anticipated another lonely place without any other believer. He took a seat on the bus, where others soon joined him. Next to him was another man of about the same age. Once the bus was under way this man started to read a book.

'Oh, so you can read,' ventured the ice cream seller.

The man smiled warmly. 'Yes, I learned at school. This is a Bible that a missionary gave me.'

'Are you a Christian, then?' asked Prichaa eagerly.

'Yes – are you?' came the rejoinder.

Soon they were talking animatedly together. To his surprise, Prichaa found that his acquaintance on the bus was going to the same town as he was. 'Do you know if there are other Christians in the town?' he inquired.

'Oh yes, there are quite a few Christians – and we have a church too. When we reach the town and get off the bus, let me take you to them. They will be glad to meet you,' said his new friend. And so Prichaa found new friends, fellowship and happiness even as he learned the important lesson that God cares for and looks after His own.

Not all the missionary efforts resulted in saved lives and conversions to Christianity. Nevertheless, we missionaries in Manorom persisted in our efforts to reach the Buddhist nurses and house-helps, getting them to memorise some verses from the Bible. I thought to myself: *Even if I can't help them to understand what they're reading, if they learn the verses by heart, one day God will bring His Word back to them and they can find Him that way.* Years later I had the opportunity to go back to Manorom and I was able to see Phikun, who worked at the guest house, and she immediately quoted to me in Thai the 'memory verse' she liked best: 'Therefore, if anyone is in Christ, he is a new creation; old things have passed away; behold, all things have become new' (2 Corinthians 5:17). I still pray that these words will one day make perfect sense to her and that she may find herself a new creation in Christ.

It was around this time, in 1991, that Eddie, by now aged 65, began to have pain in his right hip. After some months he was forced to use a walking stick. Examination and X-rays showed that he was in need of a hip replacement. We said goodbye to our missionary colleagues and Thai friends and flew back to South Africa for the surgery. After preliminary urological surgery strongly advised by his orthopaedic surgeon, he had the hip replacement operation in Cape Town in November of that year. After he was discharged from hospital we needed a place to stay where there were no steps or flights of stairs while he gradually became mobile again. What we were offered was, once again, a marvellous provision from the Lord. You will remember that when we went to Thailand in 1969 we sold our home and gave away our household appliances. We had done the same when we returned to Thailand at the beginning of 1983. Now we were back in South Africa with nowhere to stay, and it is almost incredible when I think back on what happened.

Some acquaintances of a niece of mine were on the point of going overseas for an extended holiday, and told my niece that they were looking for a couple to house-sit while they were gone. She told them of our predicament and they agreed immediately to let us stay in their home. It had no steps or stairs and there was also a separate shower, which was ideal for Eddie's post-operative needs, as he was using crutches. What perfect timing. What perfect provision. We could not have wanted anything better.

After the first period of convalescence was over (and the owners of the house were due to return from their trip abroad), we were glad to be given permission by the Dutch Reformed Church mission office to stay in their missionary flats in the Strand, without paying anything. It was ideal, as there were again no steps, and because the flats were on the coastal road we had a refreshing sea breeze cooling the hot summer days. One day we were asked to go and see the man in charge of the Mission Office, Revd Kobus Thom.

When we entered his office he greeted us with warm friendship. Later on he brought up the subject of the shortage of missionary doctors in the country of Malawi and asked if we would be willing to go to the mission hospital there for three months while two of the three doctors were on leave. Immediately after asking us, he added a warning: 'You must please think this over well before you say yes, as one in three patients to be seen there has HIV/AIDS.'

I replied, for both of us, 'I don't think we need to think it over for that reason because of our age. If we were infected, then by the time the incubation period was over, we would be old and ready to go to the Lord!'

Working in Malawi was a totally different experience from working in Thailand. We were allotted a comfortable brick house with a veranda on three sides. We had a male cook called Jamesoni (the Malawians often add an 'i' to the end of their names) and a young man called Rocket to work in the vegetable garden. We had every modern convenience, comfortable beds and fans in most rooms. We worked very hard, from 7 o'clock in the morning until suppertime. Our doctor colleagues and missionary nurses were kindness itself and we lacked for nothing. I worked in the hospital every day, in outpatients and in the wards, while Eddie also had to go into the capital city, Lilongwe, once a week to hold clinics.

After we had been there for two months, while Eddie was in Lilongwe for a clinic, he suddenly thought, *Our visas were only for two months – they must be due for renewal!* So, having his passport in his pocket, he took the opportunity of being near the immigration building and got his visa renewed. Having done that, he completely forgot about it.

Finally the day came for us to return to South Africa. A colleague drove us to the airport. As we drew near to the airport buildings Eddie said agitatedly, 'Nico, please wait here in case there is a difficulty. I renewed my own visa and completely forgot to renew Dorothy's!'

Nico parked nearby and entered the building to watch the proceedings from downstairs. With trepidation we approached the immigration officer. Eddie put our passports down on the table before the officer, making sure that his passport was on top. The officer opened Eddie's passport and checked all the pages to see that it was in order. Satisfied, he replaced it on the table and took up mine. As he looked through the passport his face grew very serious. 'This passport has only a visa for two months. It is now out of date!' he said.

Quick as a flash, Eddie replied, 'You see, we've been working in Thailand, and there, women don't count. I completely forgot to renew my wife's visa!'

The man looked up and grinned, immediately understanding Eddie's reason for the omission. 'You can go through to the departure lounge,' he said amiably. What a narrow escape we'd had!

When we came back from Malawi we settled down in George, ready to retire. But we were not left in peace for long. One of the three ministers of our church, the George Moederkerk,[1] came to visit us and when, during our conversation, we spoke a lot about our years in Thailand, he asked us how much it would cost for the church to send out missionaries of its own.

---

[1] George Mother Church.

'We can speak only about costs in Thailand,' I told him.

'That will be fine,' he replied.

We heard nothing for about a week. Then the senior minister came to visit and asked us if we would be willing to go back to Thailand once again as missionaries sent and supported by the church. 'You'd act as the vanguard,' he said. 'Once we've sent you, others are sure to follow.'

We replied that we had not expected this invitation. We would pray about it and then let him have our answer.

In God's way and in His time, within a matter of months three new invitations for us to return to Thailand came by post, a few days apart. One was for us to return to work in Manorom, the second to return to work at the Prince of Songkhla University in Hat Yai, while the third was to go to work in a town called Trang, in South Thailand. We knew Manorom, of course, and also the university. In Trang, while Eddie would work in a hospital owned by the leading elder of the church there, I would teach English to the children of two Christian schools and we would both work in co-operation with the Trang Church.

We passed on these invitations to our church leadership for them to decide where they would send us. They soon replied. Manorom already had doctors (though they always needed more), and they felt that the Thai authorities should fund their own teaching staff for the university. That left Trang, and to Trang we were to go. Little did we know what it would be like – and in the end, not only was it a new place but it also gave us a new depth of experience and fresh insight into Bible teaching.

19

Just the Two of Us

We were together; no one was with us in the house, except the two of us.

(1 Kings 3:18)

We flew to Bangkok and then changed to a smaller plane to fly on to the sprawling town of Trang, over 800 kilometres further south. From the air all we could see was a blanket of green jungle that covered hills and mountains, and huge tracts of darker green that indicated the foliage of rubber trees covering valleys and flat areas. At last we saw some buildings, huddled together in the centre of the rubber plantations. There lay Trang, the capital of this southern province. We stared out of the plane's windows at the place where we were to spend the next years of our life together.

At the airport we found Dr Visart Chowchuvech waiting for us, smiling broadly in welcome. Dr Visart was the leading elder of the Trang Christian Church and the owner of the private Trang Christian Hospital. Dr Visart's driver was there to help carry our luggage and load it into the large car. It was only a short distance from Trang airport to the town and soon we were at the church. We heard that, for the time being, we were to live in a flat in the church grounds, originally meant for guest speakers. It was most convenient for Eddie that the church was next door to the hospital, as he was to work in both the hospital and the church.

The door to the flat was inconspicuous, one of several in the long building to one side of the church. Before we entered, we all took off our shoes in true Thai style, a habit that kept the floors inside clean and shining. The front door opened immediately onto a large room, with cushioned rattan chairs round a small table, two desks with upright chairs, and a curtained-off sleeping area with a huge double bed. Visart said that he could not stay as he was needed at the hospital, but before he left he told us that he would arrange to send us our meals twice a day from the hospital kitchen. When Visart had gone, Eddie and I explored further. Passing through the bedroom's inner door, we came to a small room with two chairs and a table, on which stood a small hotplate and a kettle and cups. At the other end of the room there was no door; it passed directly to a large toilet and ablution area, walls and floor covered in white tiles. It was divided into three sections by shoulder-high tiled walls. One section had a flat, Thai cement toilet with a container of water and dish for flushing by hand. The second was for showering, with an outlet in the middle of the tiled floor, which sloped gently towards the opening. I went further into this area.

'Look, Eddie,' I called. 'Look at the shower!'

Eddie came and gazed at the showerhead with me. It was only four and a half feet above the floor. He said with a slight smile, 'Guess I'll have to kneel when I take a shower!' (He is six foot two inches tall.)

'I can't find a basin or sink anywhere,' I wailed. 'Where will we wash our crockery?'

I went into the third section of this area, to find an upturned bucket with an enamel basin balanced on top of it. There was no tap in this section.

'This must double as a sink. I can fill the basin with water from the tap alongside the shower,' I said, pleased that, however crudely, it would be possible to wash dishes in the flat.

Trang is a very large, bustling town. When we discovered that we were the only Westerners in this place of seething humanity our hearts sank initially, as we could not yet understand the Southern Thai dialect commonly spoken. This was as hard for us to understand as the broadest Glaswegian in Scotland. At first we felt it would not be possible to adapt to this dialect, but eventually we did so. As we had discovered in Hat Yai, Southern Thai is spoken very rapidly, with words being shortened in a type of spoken shorthand, and tones are often opposite to the ones we were originally taught. Years before, the OMF's Thai Language Supervisor in Bangkok, Dorothy Mainhood, had to travel to South Thailand. When she first heard people there speaking in their dialect, she could not understand them either, and thought they were speaking Malay (Malaysia borders on the southern peninsula of Thailand and many Malays have settled here).

It was hotter and more humid in Trang than we had ever experienced in other parts of Thailand. This was largely because the town was situated in a valley in the centre of a sea of rubber plantations and surrounded on all sides by mountains. This geographical feature also affected the duration and intensity of the rainy season, which lasted for eight months of the year. Each year there were floods both in the centre of town and in the outlying suburbs, as the monsoon swept in from the south-west, laden with moisture from the Indian Ocean, which it delivered as a deluge on the western boundary of South Thailand.

We had never before lived and worked in Thailand completely on our own, without other Western colleagues within reach. In Manorom we had had many other missionary doctors and nurses about us. In Hat Yai and in Songkhla we had also had Western colleagues, with whom we could have fellowship. In the early months in Trang, before I had made new Thai friends, I found myself writing often to my two good friends in South Africa, Winsome Campbell and Betty Dargin. I poured out my heart to them, telling them of our circumstances there and describing to them our feelings of isolation, asking them to pray especially for us in Trang.

Girls from the hospital kitchen came to our tiny flat twice a day at lunch and supper times, bearing a stainless-steel layered *binto*.[1] The Thai cuisine was delicious and we looked forward to these meals with gusto. Only once or twice did we return the *binto* with food uneaten. One meal we heartily disliked was a certain type of curry, *gang sôm*.[2] Fortunately that was rarely served. Once Eddie and I sat at the little table ready for supper and said grace before opening the *binto*. We were really hungry that evening and we eagerly opened the top section. But what did we find? Our

---

[1] A food carrier with three or four sections, one on top of the other.

[2] A curry that is extremely tart and raw to the Western taste.

hunger all but disappeared when we found three little sil-
ver fish, looking still very much alive as they 'swam' in the
clear liquid of a soup. The fish were even floating the right
way up! I knew I could never put one of them in my mouth,
let alone swallow it.

Dr Visart said we were not to worry about our temporary
accommodation at the church flat, as he would look for a
more permanent place for us. A few weeks later he invited
us to go with him to look at a place that might be a possibility. This was part of a building that was very conveniently
situated – on the other side of the street from the hospital
and diagonally opposite the church. It was true that it was
very convenient, but its appearance was most depressing –
a square, blackened cement building with only one or two
small, high windows. Inside we saw that it was a single,
enormous, very dark room with cement floor and dirty
walls. From one side of the room to the other there ran an
open slimy-looking gutter, with a thin stream of water
trickling along sluggishly. This gutter was evidently for slops
and emptying dregs, and the thought repelled me. My heart
sank like a stone. Was *this* where the Lord wanted us to
live? Would I live in this sordid place – for Him? I found
myself praying with earnest desperation: *Dear Lord, do You
really want us to live here? Please help me to be willing!* In the
end, it was not necessary to force myself to live there after
all. Visart said he would continue to look for more acceptable accommodation for us.

We had been in Trang only a matter of weeks when one
Sunday morning, at about 9.20, the pastor of the church,
Acharn Pornsuang, came to our flat unexpectedly. He was
due to take one of the three regular adult Sunday school

classes for new converts at 9.30. His voice gruff, he explained that he could not take the class as he had a very sore throat, and he asked Eddie to take his class on Romans 6 in his place. This sudden request took Eddie completely by surprise. It dawned on him that he would have to teach in Thai, completely unprepared. Nevertheless, he accepted graciously and in faith trusted the Lord to help him in this time of need. And the Lord helped him indeed.

One afternoon Visart came to call for us by car, inviting us to come and see a possible place for us to stay. His driver, Naaj Samer,[3] took the three of us to Nattaluang, a suburb of Trang about four miles away from the church. When we arrived we found a small townhouse, much more acceptable to our Western taste. Built of concrete, it had two floors, the downstairs part consisting of a lounge/living area, kitchen and a small box room. Upstairs there was a large bedroom with a shower and Western toilet. We assured Visart that we would be happy and grateful to live there. And so he signed the contract for a year. Before we had really come to terms with the move, we were installed in this townhouse. Visart even had his driver bring down a car for Eddie to drive. He owned twelve cars! These ranged from a 1937 left-hand-drive Chevrolet to a modern, sleek Mitsubishi. Throughout his life, Visart had never sold or traded in a car when he bought a new one. His two drivers were also excellent mechanics, and they were able to keep all the cars in serviceable condition.

The townhouses on either side of ours, identical in construction, were very close. We were glad to be so near to our

---

[3] Mr Always.

Thai neighbours, as in speaking to them our own Southern
Thai dialect improved. For a long time we were the only
Christians in our street – in the entire suburb, in fact. Our
neighbours were friendly and kind, and even appreciated
that we had a different religion. Once I was in the next-door
house and the lady there offered me some fruit to take
home. As I reached out to accept it gratefully, she took it
back in haste, remembering that it had been offered to idols
and thinking we would not be able to eat it.

While Eddie was to work in the hospital, I was not
expected to do so except for very occasional emergency
anaesthetics. Instead it had been arranged that I would
teach at two different Christian schools – one primary and
the other secondary. I was to teach English: spoken, reading
and comprehension. The children knew sufficient grammar
but lacked self-confidence in speaking. Visart arranged for a
driver to pick me up from our home before 8 a.m. and to
take me first to the primary school for a couple of lessons,
and then on to the secondary school. He would take me
home again after the afternoon classes, and I would get
back between 5 and 6 p.m. Having no textbooks to help
prepare the lessons was a challenge indeed, all the more
because I had no formal training as a teacher. But in listening to the pupils I found I picked up the commonest pitfalls
in their speaking and devised lessons to help them overcome these difficulties. For practice in comprehension I
used the Bible or other Christian books, trusting that as a
pupil read and the others listened, the message of the gospel
would be heard and understood. In the senior school alone
I taught 255 pupils in various classes. I was also required to
supply a curriculum for the two most senior classes to

matriculation standard, as well as to set and mark their final examinations. After some months I was asked by the Governor of Songkhla Province to teach English to his two teenage children. I agreed readily, and they came to our home twice weekly in the early evenings. Notwithstanding the fact that I was not a qualified teacher, I thanked God for helping me to do this work in an acceptable manner. I knew my teaching was acceptable because when Eddie and I left Trang, the headmistress, *Acharn* Marisee, refused to appoint another missionary who had applied to take my place, saying that no one could replace me!

With some of the money that our church in South Africa supplied quarterly we bought a washing machine from a shop whose owner, according to Dr Visart, was sympathetic to Christians. It was a tremendous help to me during these busy days. I would start a washing cycle before 6 a.m. and would hang it outside before I left for the schools. During the months that brought monsoon rains to Trang I would have to hang the washing indoors, with a fan trained on the clothes. This fan often had to be left on non-stop for two days and nights at a time before the washing was sufficiently dry, because of the 100 per cent humidity that prevailed all the year round. Even the continuous intense heat could not overcome the extreme humidity.

All the time we lived in our townhouse we were invaded by scorpions and centipedes, with occasional snakes outside the house. Some liked to sunbathe on top of the back wall; others left their calling cards in the form of a cast-off skin just outside our back door. These invaders came from the rubber plantations that stretched for miles on the other side of our back wall. The scorpions were small but deadly, and

I hated them. Even when we showered we would often find we were sharing the small space with a scorpion that had crept in through a hole in one of the ventilation airbricks. I had never ever expected to be standing, undressed, right next to a scorpion!

One Sunday morning I came downstairs early, while it was still dark. I was barefoot, as we did not wear shoes indoors. I reached for the light switch and turned on the lights. My heart skipped a beat or two as I sensed a movement near my feet. I looked down and saw a scorpion, tail raised and curved, moving towards me. In God's protection, however, we were never stung.

After I had prepared breakfast that same Sunday I called Eddie to come and eat, and then we washed the dishes. Then it was time to drive to the church for the morning worship service. Eddie got into the car while I fetched a Bible from the bookcase downstairs, tucking it under my arm. I gave him the Bible once I was inside the car. As he took it from me, he shot out of his seat to stand next to the car, shaking the Bible to let out the scorpion whose tail he had seen protruding from between the pages! This prompted Eddie to point out that it was another more amusing interpretation of the verse, 'The word of God is living. . .' (Hebrews 4:12). More seriously, of course, it had been God's love and protection that stopped the scorpion from emerging while I was carrying the Bible under my arm, and I thanked Him then and there.

Eddie enjoyed working in Visart's hospital, as he was free to tell patients of God's love and healing as he worked. Surgery was not a major part of his work, because the hospital was small and the equipment not really suited to major operative work. One morning a patient was brought into his consulting room in a wheelchair. He could not walk because of severe pain in both knees. Immediately Eddie sent him for X-rays. When he saw the finished plates, which showed a great deal of deterioration and degeneration in the bones of both knee joints, Eddie went back to the patient and told him he could not help him as both knees needed replacement surgery. But the patient expostulated, saying he had heard of other patients with painful knees whom Eddie had helped greatly by injections into the knee. He wanted Eddie to inject his knees also. Eddie tried to explain to the patient that treatment by injection was not indicated for his knees as they were very badly affected, but the patient insisted vehemently that Eddie should perform the injections. Against his better judgement, Eddie complied and injected cortisone with local anaesthetic, telling the man not to expect too much in the way of improvement as his knees were already too far gone for an injection to do much good.

The following day, Eddie was sitting in his examination room waiting for the next patient to come in when a man walked into the room. 'Good morning, doctor,' he said.

Eddie greeted him and the patient sat down in the chair in front of the desk. For a short time there was silence, and then the man spoke again. 'Don't you remember me, doctor?' he asked. 'I am the man whose knees you injected. Thank you very much! My knees are much better. I've come to you to have another injection!'

Eddie's thoughts raced back to the crippled patient in his wheelchair and he opened his eyes wide with wonder at the startling improvement in his condition. 'I can't give you another injection now,' he said. 'It's still too soon. You will have to wait another two weeks at least before I can inject your knees again.' Eddie then seized on the opportunity that had presented itself, and went on, 'I want you to know that it's not me whom you should thank, but God! We doctors do what we can. We treat our patients and operate on them when it's necessary. But *whatever* we do it's never enough by itself – it's God Himself who actually causes healing of tissues. I did what I could by injecting your knees, but it's God who has made them so much better!'

The man listened intently and accepted a copy of John's Gospel that was lying on the desk, promising to read it. He left the hospital and did not return – at least, not while Eddie was still working there – so evidently his improvement remained.

We marvelled at the way Dr Visart's drivers kept his fleet of cars roadworthy, even though some were at least 50 years old. The car that Visart lent to Eddie to use while we were in Trang was old, but rarely gave us any trouble. A noteworthy exception, though, occurred one day while we were travelling to Hat Yai, about 160 kilometres away.

We left our house early that morning as we had several things we needed to do in Hat Yai. Even so, we were not early enough to avoid the many cars of the morning rush hour, bustling crowds of pedestrians, cyclists and motorcyclists vying for position on the overcrowded streets. We passed restaurants with their rickety tables and stools arranged on the pavement outside, all filled with people eating *batangkaw*[4] that had been dipped into condensed

---

[4] Small fried pieces of dough.

milk and drinking small tumblers of sweet, milky coffee – a favourite breakfast snack in Thailand. The Trang open market area was thronged with housewives buying fresh meat, fruit and vegetables for that day. Through the car's open windows came an unpleasant odour of fish, crabs and other shellfish from one area of the market. On the counters of open-fronted little shops we could see black bananas, tempting the passers-by. The bananas had been boiled in their skins while still not ripe and this had turned them black and shiny.

After about 15 minutes we left the town behind us as our road began to climb through the jungle-clad mountains that surrounded Trang. While we were negotiating this winding, steep road, Eddie gestured towards the dashboard where a red light had begun to glow. Our engine had started to overheat. This was a lonely stretch of road, with no sign of human habitation. I grew anxious, but Eddie calmed me down, saying that he thought he remembered a few wooden houses fairly nearby and he thought he could nurse the car gently until we reached these houses, where we would be able to get some water for the (obviously leaking) radiator. We went on slowly, looking all the while for any signs of houses, but in vain. The temperature climbed higher and higher. The road was too narrow to turn around and, in any case, it was too far to coast back to Trang. Above us on the left was the steep side of the mountain, with the unbroken green of luxuriant jungle on the slope to the right. I prayed silently, even as the needle of the temperature gauge crept higher and higher.

Suddenly Eddie exclaimed, 'Dos, look! There, on the right, down in the valley! Aren't those buildings down there?'

I looked and there they were, a settlement of some sort with one or two weathered wooden shacks. Within a few metres, Eddie spotted a narrow dirt road leading off ours and we turned right to follow it. When we arrived at the shacks he stopped the car and we got out, calling to let the people know we were there. But no one answered. A forlorn, tattered garment hung on a clothes line, where it had clearly been forgotten in the departure of the people who had lived there. What were we to do? We needed water for the car's radiator, desperately. Then Eddie made a find. He had seen a tap sticking out above a clump of long grasses. Gingerly, he turned it on. A moderate stream of water emerged. We could not help smiling at each other. But as quickly as we rejoiced over our find, our hearts sank again. With no one around, we could not ask for a bucket or a jug to pour the water into the radiator.

We cast about desperately, among the accumulation of rubbish and waste on the ground. When we found a small, empty condensed milk tin with its lid gaping wide we were relieved and pleased – until we realised just how long it would take us to fill the car's radiator with it. While Eddie started the tedious process I still looked around, but found only a very small bottle, which would be of less use than the tin. At last, hidden in the long grass, Eddie spied a length of narrow green plastic hose. Gleefully he picked it up and found it was long enough to reach from the tap to the radiator. He filled the radiator and soon we were ready to drive off once more.

Rather than turn the car around and go back to the pass where we had turned off it, we considered an alternative: Eddie had seen that the old road we were on continued along the valley and he knew that it would lead us back to the pass, but much further on. We almost went on that way. If we had, it would have led to disaster indeed, but the Lord kept us safe, in His providence. While Eddie had been searching the deserted grounds for a receptacle for water, he had noticed that this old road led to a wooden bridge across a small ravine. As he looked further now, however, he noticed that part of the wooden beams supporting the bridge had rotted away. If we had not had to search the area so closely, he would not have noticed the state of the bridge in time and we would have tumbled to our deaths at the bottom of the ravine. Surely the Lord had answered our prayers.

The rest of the trip to Hat Yai was uneventful. As soon as we arrived we looked out for a car repair shop, of which there were many. Eddie parked alongside a small one and told the mechanic of our problem with the leaking radiator. 'No problem!' he reassured us. 'Just drive up on the pavement here and we will fix it for you.'

Eddie did as he asked and soon the mechanic and his assistant were busy with the radiator, their welding equipment stretching along the pavement. They had soon repaired the leak. The cost? The incredibly small sum of 20 baht (less than 1 US dollar). We learned that day about the marvellous ingenuity of the Thai. Although the mechanics had no garage or space to work on cars, they were not hampered. They simply used the pavement, while pedestrians nonchalantly stepped into the street to give them room. We realised that day that in spite of climatic drawbacks, Thailand has some particular advantages over the West!

20

Triumph in Trang

To declare the name of the LORD in Zion,
And His praise in Jerusalem,
When the peoples are gathered together,
And the kingdoms, to serve the LORD.
(Psalm 102:21–22)

On our first Sunday morning in Trang, Eddie and I left our small flat to go to church. The nearer we got, the louder was the happy sound of singing and clapping that came through the open door. This was something new to us, as in South Africa we had become accustomed to a quieter, more reverent service.

Inside, we found a crowd of about 200 worshippers. We managed to find two empty seats and joined in the hearty singing. Of course the words to the choruses were in Thai, but they were projected on a screen and that made it easy for us. We knew all the tunes, which lessened the feeling of being alone in a sea of Thai. *I wonder whether I'll ever be able to adjust to this kind of worshipping?* was the thought that flashed through my mind. But fortunately my concern was short lived. After about 20 minutes of the boisterous singing the character of the choruses changed gradually to quieter and more worshipful songs. Sometime later I learned that this was usual, as it allowed latecomers to straggle into the church without disrupting the service. 'What a young man!' I whispered to Eddie as the minister, *Acharn* Pornsuang, climbed the steps to the platform in the front. 'Shhh!' hissed Eddie.

I dutifully kept quiet and listened to the preacher's words. In spite of his youth Pornsuang was spiritually mature, and his sermon was both challenging and moving. As we got to know him we found Pornsuang an inspiration. He was a great leader. The church in Trang was an oasis of Christianity in that dark land of bondage and spirit worship. We were amazed at the depth and vigour of spiritual life in that church, which had been without a missionary for over 70 years.

On Sundays, the church's schedule started at 8.30 a.m. with an hour of Sunday school. After that there was an hour of classes for new believers, taken by Pornsuang and two senior elders. Then came the worship service, until noon, after which the members made their way to an area at the back of the church grounds where they would eat together. The meal was prepared by some of the older women and served at rough wooden tables by teenagers. The young people also cleared the tables and washed the dishes. Even when the meal was finished, the church's activities were not yet over: in the afternoons some women would visit the sick in hospital, while others went to the homes of any who had not attended church for a long time.

When we had finished eating, a young man came up to us, a friendly smile on his face. 'I'm glad to meet you,' he said. 'I'm Tirayut, the assistant pastor. I studied at Bangkok Bible College at the same time as *Acharn* Pornsuang. I hope you will be very happy here in Trang. We are glad to have you with us.'

We were impressed with this keen young man, who was obviously as dedicated as Pornsuang himself to the Lord's service. As we spoke together we found he had a very quick mind and wit. This is illustrated by a story he told us of his time at the college in Bangkok.

'While we were students there,' he said, 'a friend of mine was not convinced that the theory of evolution was not true. I didn't know how to explain to him what I felt, that God created the earth and all that is in it, and evolution alone could not explain the wonders of the creation. But then one day he came into my little room, where I was studying. A globe-shaped paperweight on my table caught his eye, and he asked, "Who made this?" Immediately I replied, "It just happened!" I hoped that my words would let him understand just how ridiculous it was that the entire universe and everything in it simply evolved by itself!'

Tirayut's dedication and devotion to the Lord were never more evident than when he proposed to his girlfriend, Petcharat. When he was the leader of the weekly cell group near our home, he told us that he had said, 'Petcharat, I love you very much, but I have to tell you that there is Someone I love more!'

One Sunday morning, in the middle of the service, there was a sudden hush. The woman leader for that morning, Jiamchit, stopped in the middle of giving out the notices for the week. Eddie saw others in the congregation turning their heads to the centre aisle, so he did the same. Then he nudged me to look in that direction too. We could never have dreamed of what we saw – a largish black bat was slowly making its way up the aisle! It teetered from side to side as it used the points of its folded wings to keep itself upright. It turned neither to the left nor to the right as it continued resolutely up to the platform at the front of the church. Then, without further ado, it turned right round and made its way down the central aisle and out of the church. Moments after the creature disappeared through the door, the service resumed where it had been interrupted.

One Sunday, immediately after *Acharn* Pornsuang finished preaching, a little old lady stood up at the back of the church and walked diffidently up the aisle. She asked Pornsuang if she might be allowed to give a testimony of what the Lord meant to her. Pornsuang nodded, and she turned round to face the congregation.

'I have been a Christian for only a short time,' she began. 'Even so, God has been very good to me in my life and I would like to tell you all about it.' Her voice was soft and gentle – speaking in public was obviously strange to her. She continued, 'Three nights ago I was sleeping on my mat on the floor of my home. I was tired, so when I felt something heavy lying on top of my legs I hardly woke up. I knew it was our cat, because she often disturbs us by coming to sleep next to us when the nights are cooler. I wriggled to get her off me and went to sleep again, but then felt this weight again, now on my chest. I moved away from the weight, but it stayed on my chest. By now I was fully awake and I opened my eyes. I found I could see in the faint light before the dawn. But as I looked, I saw a terrible thing! Right in front of my eyes was the raised, hooded head of a king cobra, swaying from side to side and ready to strike. My mind froze. I couldn't think what to do! The only thing I could do was to shout out, "*Jesus*!" And the snake, unbelievably, lowered its threatening head, slid off my body and slithered out of the window. My husband is also a Christian. He quickly followed the snake outside and killed it. I wanted to tell you what happened so you all can know too what a mighty Lord we have!'

After the old lady finished speaking there was silence for a minute or two. Then the entire congregation spontaneously clapped their hands and fervently said, 'Amen!' Instead of announcing a hymn to close the service, Pornsuang chose rather a chorus of praise to the Lord. That was indeed a memorable Sunday!

There was no organ in the church, but to the left at the front was a grand piano. 'Why a piano and not an organ?' we asked Jo, Pornsuang's wife.

'We don't like organ music!' she replied. 'I play the piano for the young people's choir.'

When we had been in Trang for some months, Pornsuang discovered that Eddie could play the piano, and that as long as the tune was familiar, he did not need music. Then Pornsuang decided that Eddie should play during the Sunday services along with the electric guitars, drums and keyboard. This proved difficult and disconcerting at first, as, without any warning, the other players would switch keys and leave Eddie nonplussed. But later Pornsuang arranged a weekly practice. Just before a key change, the bass guitarist, standing nearest to the piano, would shout a quick warning so that Eddie could change harmonies in time.

Pornsuang asked Eddie to train the young people's choir.

Jo played the piano, while I turned pages. Soon the Governor of Trang Province heard of the choir and invited them to perform at his mansion. When Eddie found that the Governor had no piano he tried to turn down the invitation, but he insisted that the choir perform for him. Just in time we found a solution: Eddie had a tape that included the pieces to be sung. He arranged that I should sit next to the tape recorder so that I could adjust the volume – loud when the choir sang, and soft or mute in between. I found this nerve-racking and even had nightmares in which I made a mistake. The orchestral backing on the tape, however, made the singing sound most professional and the Governor and his wife were very pleased with the choir's performance (even though they were staunch Buddhists and the lyrics were all Christian).

The two most important times for Trang Church were Easter and Christmas. At Easter there was a unique gathering in the town's cemetery on Easter Sunday. The service began early, at 6 a.m. Everyone gathered among the graves where Christians had been buried, adjoining the Chinese burial area. Everybody was smiling as they greeted each other. A sense of rejoicing spread through the crowd. First we sang triumphant Easter hymns and then Pornsuang addressed the crowd with an amplifier powered by a car's battery. 'You see these gravestones?' he asked. 'These people all died in Christ, and they are not here! Oh yes, their graves are here and their bodies lie in the earth, but they themselves are with God, to live for ever more!' His words were punctuated with cracks and bangs of fireworks from the adjoining Chinese cemetery. The fireworks were intended to ward off evil spirits. Every now and again some

Chinese mourners would lift their heads to listen to Porn-suang's words. What a contrast there was between them and the jubilant, triumphant Christians.

We learned that on Christmas Day the church and its large grounds were open to the public from early morning. Eddie and I went there at 8.30. Already some hundreds of visitors milled about the grounds, eyes darting here and there, curious about what these Christians did. Some were watching biblical plays put on either by Sunday school children or the church's teenagers, and we watched, too, for a while. We grew peckish and joined others lining up at stalls scattered around, serving food and soft drinks. By mid-morning the visitors numbered well over 1,000, so you can imagine what difficulty the women of the church had in preparing food for them. They were well aware that the Thai generally eat when they are hungry and are not governed by the clock, so they had anticipated that some would want breakfast while others would want lunch. Later on in the morning the crowds started gathering for the Christmas service in the church itself. Obviously the church was too small for all the people, so the overflow streamed to the tented areas that had been erected on either side of the church, where large screens showed the service on closed-circuit television.

While we were living in the townhouse, the water supply would simply stop without warning for an hour or two, so we prepared for these times by keeping buckets filled with water in the shower-cum-toilet. One morning I came downstairs early to start a load of washing in time to hang it out before I left for school. I had just started the machine, and was about to go back upstairs, when suddenly the sound of water rushing in through the inlet pipe ceased. *Oh, no! I thought. I must get this washing done. Why has the water stopped right now?* And I hesitated, with my foot already on the first stair. Without thinking about it I shut my eyes and prayed, *Dear Lord, I really need to get this washing done this morning before I have to leave. Please, please help me! You are my Father and I am Your child. I know that You love me. I plead with You to intervene!* And while I was standing there, riveted by my heart's cry, I heard the rushing sound of the water start again. How I praised the Lord for coming to my aid in such a practical, down-to-earth manner!

One year, just a week before Christmas, our water was cut off for a fortnight. How were we to manage? We knew we could fetch drinking water from Visart's hospital, but we also desperately needed water for cooking, showering and laundry. I ran next door and spoke to our neighbour, Mrs Pichet. 'Is your water also off?' I asked her.

'Oh, yes,' she said. 'This happens to us at Nattaluang every few years. You see, no politician or important person lives in this suburb. When the authorities need to shut down the water supply to a suburb to save the more important suburbs, they always seem to choose Nattaluang.'

'But what can we do?' I asked, distraught.

'Don't worry,' she comforted me. 'You know the school nearby, along the main road?' I nodded. 'They have a well in their grounds, and we can fetch water from the well. We don't even have to pay for the water!'

Mrs Pichet was right. After a few days we became accustomed to fetching and storing water in containers, either from the hospital or from the well at the school, where sometimes long queues formed.

That year Christmas Day was on a Sunday. Eddie and I went to the church at 8.30 a.m. and already there were crowds of well over 1,000 people milling about the grounds. A festive spirit spread through them and everyone was smiling and laughing. Everyone was polite to each other. We nodded to acquaintances and chatted to friends in between watching some of the ingenious plays that were performed on makeshift platforms. Suddenly Eddie stopped short, his face showing his distress.

'Dos, I've left my camera at home!' he said. 'I must get some shots of the crowd and also the decorations in the church. Then I can show people at home what Christmas means to the people of Trang.'

'But it's late,' I said. 'You'll never get back in time for the church service.'

'No, I must go. I think I can just make it,' he assured me – and with that he was gone, swallowed up in the crowd.

I kept an eye on my watch as the hands crept inexorably towards the scheduled start of the service, but no Eddie appeared. It was only when the service was already beginning that he appeared, sliding into his place beside me, carrying his camera. 'I'll tell you what happened after the service!' he whispered urgently, under cover of the preliminary singing.

As soon as the service was over, Eddie turned to me. 'You won't believe what happened when I got home!'

'I'm just glad you made it back in time,' I countered.

'No, Dos, just listen! I know why I had this feeling that I must fetch the camera even though it was late: God was urging me to go.' His face was alight with exhilaration. 'When I reached our house there was a water tanker in the road, just about ready to leave. I got out and called to the driver not to go, and he waited for me. I got every container I could out of the house and filled them with water. *Khun* Pichet's youngsters ran over and helped me carry the heavy buckets into the house and upstairs. We've got lots of water now!'

Was it merely coincidence that made Eddie insist on fetching his camera at the very time that the water truck was still at Nattaluang? No. I believe it was the Lord's prompting. And because he went, we now had enough water in the house to last us for days, without needing to lug each bucketful from the well.

Whenever a member of the church died, a wake was held in the early evening in the area at the back of the church grounds where the wooden tables and benches were. Pornsuang always asked Eddie to play the keyboard, which had been brought from the church. In front was a platform, beautifully decorated with tropical flowers. There were huge vases of flowers on each side and strands of flowers hung from the top. In the middle of the platform, supported on a trestle, lay the open coffin. To the left a large framed photograph of the deceased was displayed. Once, when we attended the wake of an old woman, we found it strange that the photo on display was of a woman in her twenties.

'Why is the picture of a young woman?' we asked the man sitting next to us.

'But of course, the photo is of her when she was converted,' he replied. And when we thought about it, of course we agreed that such a picture was most suitable, as it showed her at the time she had received eternal life in Jesus Christ.

After a hymn and a prayer, people took it in turns to climb up to the platform, where a family member would pass them a plastic bottle of scent and they would spray scent over the body before passing the bottle to a person waiting on the other side of the platform. This solemn procession was orderly; the oldest went first and the children last. After everyone had taken his or her turn, the coffin was sealed. After the wake was over, it was buried in the Christian part of the Trang cemetery. Pornsuang then gave the funeral address, which always included a gospel message, as there were always Buddhist family members present too. The service closed with another hymn, after which all the young people present rose to set the tables and serve everybody with a sumptuous meal. The family of the deceased would bear the cost – not a small thing, as often hundreds attended the wakes. This explained why most wakes lasted only three or four days, while a few lasted for seven. The length obviously depended on the wealth of the family.

Trang Church has several 'daughter churches' in smaller villages nearby, just as keen as the larger church in Trang itself. Whenever there was a wedding or a funeral wake in one of these smaller churches, members from Trang would go by chartered bus or van to encourage them by their presence. Trang Church is also responsible for bi-monthly gatherings out in the surrounding jungle, where the gospel is preached and people can hear of the salvation there is to be found by faith in Christ.

Because Malaysia is nearby, a good number of Muslims live in South Thailand. Once while we were there, a group of Muslim men travelled from another town in order to see

Acharn Pornsuang. He was most surprised when he heard that they had come to ask the Christians in Trang to pray for the recovery of a boy in his teens who had suddenly become dumb. Pornsuang assured the men that he and the members of the church would pray for the boy's recovery, warning them at the same time that prayer was not like putting money in a slot machine. It was startling to us that these Muslims had brought themselves to the point of asking Christians for help. It was unheard of in Thailand for such an approach to be made. No one ever came back to us to tell us what happened to the boy, but having committed him to the Lord, we felt all would be well.

Pornsuang's attitude to the collection of money at church services was both novel and inspirational. When the time came for him to announce the collection of the day's thank offering, he would say, 'We are now going to collect our thank offering to the Lord. Those of you who do not yet know the Lord, please do not feel that you should contribute to the offering. It is taken as a sign of gratitude to God, given with free will by His children.' We had never heard a minister say that to a congregation before!

Seven years before our arrival in Trang, the leaders of the church had started a building fund. We could see that the present building would soon be too small. Each Sunday between 200 and 250 people gathered for worship, and there was hardly any room for additional worshippers.

'Why don't you start building now?' Eddie asked. 'You have plenty of ground available, and you can go on collecting funds to pay off the money you borrow.'

'No, we won't do that,' was Pornsuang's reply. 'We will not incur debt. That will not be honouring God. We plan to collect sufficient money first, however long it takes, before we start the building.'

Eddie and I left Thailand to retire in 1995, before the building fund had grown sufficiently to start building the new church. We have remained in constant e-mail contact with Thai friends, and so were able to follow the progress of the building project even though we were now far away. In October 1999 came a wonderful gift from our 'spiritual daughter', Kok-Tow, whom we had got to know and love when we were in Hat Yai. She had moved to Florida, USA, and longed to support the Lord's work financially and with prayer. Because of her gift to us we were able to fly to Thailand for a short visit to Trang. Fortunately our visit included a Sunday, and so we had the privilege of sharing in the morning worship service with 400 others in the beautiful new church. There was still ample room for more, as the new building was large enough to accommodate 1,000 people. It also had air conditioning, not only for comfort in the prevailing heat and high humidity, but also to eliminate the noise of traffic from the busy road adjacent to the church.

What a joy it was for us to receive such a loving welcome! All the faces were wreathed in beaming smiles as they waited to have a word with us. The Thai people characteristically smile a lot, and one well-known name for Thailand is 'The Land of Smiles'. But these smiles were really out of the ordinary. People's faces lit up with heavenly joy as they experienced the presence of the Lord Jesus Christ. We thanked God for the unshakeable witness of these, His people, and renewed our commitment to pray for them daily.

Epilogue

And everyone who has left houses or brothers or
sisters or father or mother or wife or children or
lands, for My name's sake, shall receive a hun-
dred-fold, and inherit eternal life.

(Matthew 19:29)

The Thai whom we had got to know and love during
our missionary years are still dear to us and have
become family to us. We long to see them and
encourage them from time to time. After our brief return to
Thailand in 1999, which included short visits to Manorom
and Trang, our appetite was whetted for more such trips.
Unfortunately, my health has deteriorated and it is not possible for me to repeat such a journey in the foreseeable
future.

Towards the end of March 2003 we learned that Dr Visart
was suffering from a malignant lymphoma and that the
chemotherapy had to be stopped because of a very bad reaction. That night Eddie could not sleep. He tossed and
turned, the faces of Visart and his wife Lumchuan ever
before him in recurring dreams. Then he started to dream
about other people in Trang. He longed to see them again,

even though he would have to go there without me. In his half-asleep state he then realised that any overseas trip at that time was out of the question, as our passports were still with the Home Office, where we had sent them together with our applications for permanent residence in the UK. In any case, our finances were not adequate for him to make a trip to Thailand at that time. In the middle of the night, as I slept peacefully alongside him, Eddie prayed earnestly, asking for encouragement from the Lord. At last his anxieties were quieted and he was at peace again. In the early hours he finally went to sleep.

He was still sleeping when the postman pushed our mail through the letterbox the next morning. I immediately noticed an important-looking envelope, bearing a stamp saying 'Home Office'. Simultaneously I heard little sounds from the bedroom. Eddie was awake. I hurried in to him with the mail, brandishing the Home Office envelope as I entered the room. 'Open this one,' I said. 'It's from the Home Office!'

Eddie sat up and took it from me, tearing open the envelope eagerly. 'Our passports are inside!' he said excitedly. 'I didn't expect them for another month or two.' He opened one and turned the pages quickly. 'Look, we've been granted permanent residence status!' We looked at each other in delight and then, in unspoken agreement, we bowed our heads and shut our eyes, to thank God for His faithfulness and love.

'What else came in the post?' Eddie asked. I had not looked at the other mail until then, so now I riffled through the envelopes, most of which were advertisements.

'Here's a letter,' I said. 'It's from Kok-Tow in America!'

The envelope was a large, heavy one. She had sent it by Global Priority Mail, taking advantage of the fact that the weight of the padded envelope did not alter the price of the postage, so she had carefully stuffed small gifts for Susan and us into it, as well as photographs of her widespread family. Inside, too, was a sealed envelope addressed to Eddie and me. Eddie opened the envelope to find a letter to us both – and a cheque for 2,000 US dollars. We were stunned. The Lord had solved both of Eddie's problems at one stroke. He lost no time in booking his flights for a nine-day trip to Thailand.

When he arrived in Trang he found Visart slightly improved and able to endure his chemotherapy again. The Thai welcomed Eddie with love and warm hospitality, and the trip was a spiritual tonic to him. He returned home laden with gifts and messages for me – *Khun mae*.[1]

Most graduates from the Prince of Songkhla University move to Bangkok, where jobs are plentiful. In April 2004, *Acharn* Pornsuang became aware of the need for a new church there for the spiritual benefit of these graduates. In order not to clash with the services of other established churches in Bangkok, the services in this new church are held on Sunday afternoons. Eddie and I received an e-mail telling us its name in Thai, *Jye-Pook-Pun* ('Hearts bound closely together'), and further rather frantic e-mails asking us to suggest a name in English that would be a good trans-lation, referring to the closeness of the members' fellow-ship. We suggested the name 'Binding Hearts Church', and the church committee accepted this. They thought it easy

---

[1] 'Mother' – the name the Thai often used for me.

for foreigners who could not speak Thai to call it the 'BHC' for short.

Different preachers lead the services at the new church, including *Acharn* Pornsuang (once or twice a month). Of course the membership of the new church was initially very small, but a short time ago we heard by e-mail that Sunday attendances are now between 80 and 100. The growth in numbers brought to our minds the time when Peter and John preached to the crowds in Jerusalem: 'But the word of God grew and multiplied' (Acts 12:24).

Dr Apithan is writing regular Bible studies for the members of the new church. He wrote to us to say the studies have to be short or no one will have time to read them! The general population, even Christians, do not have much of a habit of reading or studying. His wife Mong is training the church choir in preparation for the Christmas programme. Although Eddie will not be there to teach them this year, in his heart and in mine, too, we will be there with them – these, the spiritual children God has given us. We pray for this new church daily, 'being confident of this very thing, that He who has begun a good work in you will complete it until the day of Jesus Christ' (Philippians 1:6).

* * *

Note

After we left Trang in 1995, Eddie and I retired eventually to the UK, to be near Anthony, Jennifer and Susan and our grandchildren. David and his wife Chantelle stayed in South Africa. David, in spite of his traumatic childhood experiences, is now a lay preacher in the Methodist Church, and all four children are following the Lord.

Appendix

Overseas Missionary Fellowship

In 1865 Hudson Taylor founded the China Inland Mission in England. Compelled by the love of God and overwhelmed by the spiritual plight of the millions of Chinese lost without the Saviour, the Lord Jesus Christ, he set out for China in faith, accompanied by 24 others who shared his evangelising zeal. The CIM was a 'faith mission' – that is, it relied by faith on God's provision for the supply of its needs, rather than asking the public for donations.

At the time of the Communist takeover in China in 1949, all CIM missionaries had to leave, as their continued presence there would have endangered the lives of Chinese Christians. After having been evacuated, the missionaries continued working among Chinese people who were living in other countries in South-east Asia. In ensuing years, the name of the CIM was changed to the 'Overseas Missionary Fellowship' as its field of mission work gradually extended to include most of the peoples of South-east Asia.

OMF International has always held to Hudson Taylor's well-known tenet: 'God's work, done in God's way and in His time, will never lack supply.'